Praise for *The Heart of the M...*

"The Heart of the Matter ... wisdom, broad avenues to deep ... the book's clear and practical e... profound healing ...

by
g

— **Brian L. Weiss, M.D.**, autl... *...any Lives, Many Masters*

"The Heart of the Matter by Dr. Darren Weissman and Cate Montana just surged to the top of my recommended list. Dr. Weissman's practical, no-nonsense approach to a whole new conscious way of living is both original and attainable. Accepting his See Feel Hear Challenge will change your life! You no longer will simply have information, or, as he puts it, 'Having intellectual knowledge about something doesn't bestow wisdom any more than knowing the brain is capable of creating and releasing endorphins to mitigate pain gets rid of a headache.' Instead, you will have power— the power that is your birthright to manifest the nearly unlimited potential that resides within each and every one of us! Don't miss this one—read it today!"*

— **Eldon Taylor**, *New York Times* best-selling author of *Choices and Illusions*

"The Heart of the Matter shares techniques for changing yourself and your life that have proven effective. If you are inspired to create a new self and life, then let your desire, intention, and inspiration become guided by the information presented here, and it will become your life coach."*

— **Bernie Siegel, M.D.**, best-selling author, including *A Book of Miracles: Inspiring True Stories of Healing, Gratitude, and Love*

*"If you're ready to move to the next level of health, well-being, and a life that works, **The Heart of the Matter** can surely take you there. This outstanding book is a significant achievement in spiritual*

technology, marrying broad-stroke metaphysical truth with practical, grounded examples and techniques for healing and transformation. Follow the guidance between these covers, and your life will surely be lighter, freer, and happier."

— **Alan Cohen**, seminar leader and best-selling author of *The Dragon Doesn't Live Here Anymore*

"As a licensed psychotherapist, I am often witness to people becoming stuck in negative feelings or behavioral patterns. They want to change—they know how to change, but they keep ending up in the same place, disheartened and deflated. In this eloquently written book, Dr. Darren Weissman goes deeper with the See Feel Hear Challenge, allowing you to access the hidden subconscious emotional patterns that are running your life. This allows you to transform both physical and psychological aliments. I recommend this book and plan on using it with my clients."

— **Nicole McCance, M.A., C. Psych Assoc.**, licensed psychotherapist and best-selling author

"This is by far one of the best books on the planet for emotional healing and transformation. Apply these brilliant suggestions and enjoy the benefit of your life changing in beautiful, harmonious, and loving ways."

— **Peggy McColl**, *New York Times* best-selling author of *Your Destiny Switch*

*"**The Heart of the Matter** provides a straightforward way to quickly get to the heart of our "problems" and release old, toxic emotions and programs so we can live the joyous lives we were meant to live. I wish that I'd known this simple technique years ago!"*

— **Betsy Chasse**, filmmaker, *What the Bleep Do We Know!?;* author, *Tipping Sacred Cows*

The heart
of the Matter

ALSO BY DR. DARREN WEISSMAN

*Awakening to the Secret Code of Your Mind**

The Daily Lessons of Infinite Love & Gratitude
(children's book with B. T. Brunelle)

*The Power of Infinite Love & Gratitude**

ALSO BY CATE MONTANA

GhettoPhysics

Unearthing Venus

*Available from Hay House

Please visit:

Hay House USA: **www.hayhouse.com**®
Hay House Australia: **www.hayhouse.com.au**
Hay House UK: **www.hayhouse.co.uk**
Hay House South Africa: **www.hayhouse.co.za**
Hay House India: **www.hayhouse.co.in**

The heart

of the Matter

*A Simple Guide to Discovering Gifts
in Strange Wrapping Paper*

Dr. Darren Weissman and Cate Montana

HAY HOUSE, INC.

Carlsbad, California • New York City
London • Sydney • Johannesburg
Vancouver • Hong Kong • New Delhi

Published and distributed in the United States by: Hay House, Inc.: www.hayhouse
.com® • *Published and distributed in Australia by:* Hay House Australia Pty. Ltd.:
www.hayhouse.com.au • *Published and distributed in the United Kingdom by:* Hay
House UK, Ltd.: www.hayhouse.co.uk • *Published and distributed in the Republic of
South Africa by:* Hay House SA (Pty), Ltd.: www.hayhouse.co.za • *Distributed in Canada by:*
Raincoast: www.raincoast.com • *Published in India by:* Hay House Publishers India:
www.hayhouse.co.in

Cover design: Amy Rose Grigoriou • *Interior design:* Pamela Homan
Interior graphics: Shelley Lucas
Interior Photoshop samples: Barbra Kates Photography

Library of Congress Cataloging-in-Publication Data

Weissman, Darren R.
  The heart of the matter : a simple guide to discovering gifts in strange wrapping paper
/ Dr. Darren Weissman and Cate Montana.
     pages cm
  Includes index.
  ISBN 978-1-4019-4073-7 (tradepaper : alk. paper) 1. Mind and body. 2. Self-actualiza-
tion (Psychology) 3. Self-perception. I. Montana, Cate. II. Title.
  BF161.W393 2013
  158--dc23
                                    2013003162

Tradepaper ISBN: 978-1-4019-4073-7

16 15 14 13   5 4 3 2
1st edition, September 2013
2nd edition, September 2013

Printed in the United States of America

SUSTAINABLE
FORESTRY
INITIATIVE
Certified Chain of Custody
Promoting Sustainable Forestry
www.sfiprogram.org
SFI-01268
SFI label applies to the text stock

CONTENTS

PART I: What Is the Heart of the Matter?

PART II: How and Why It Works

PART III: Challenges to Choosing a Purposeful Life

PART IV: Creating Conscious Change

FOREWORD

"[T]he stream of knowledge is heading towards a non-mechanical reality; the universe begins to look more like a great thought than like a great machine. Mind no longer appears as an accidental intruder into the realm of matter. . . . We ought rather to hail it as the creator and governor of the realm of matter."

— SIR JAMES JEANS, 1930

In 1925, quantum physics revolutionized our understanding of the mechanics of the world, revealing that the entire universe is made out of one thing: *energy*. The principles of quantum mechanics emphasized that the human mind and consciousness, interacting with the energy field of the universe, profoundly shape our experience of reality.

Scientists and laypeople didn't readily adopt this scientific fact. Finding it difficult to accept this hypothesis in the face of a reality where our lives rarely match the wishes and desires of our minds, we preferred to labor under the perception that life was controlled by "outside" forces.

All that's about to change. A scientific renaissance offered by the frontier sciences of epigenetics and quantum biophysics reveals a *new* biology that further challenges our persistent assumptions that we are "victims" of life. The new science illuminates the mechanisms by which the environment, and, more specifically, the mind's *perception* of the environment, controls our life experiences.

The primary function of the mind is to orchestrate our behavior to create coherence between our beliefs and the reality we experience. This power of the mind is best displayed in onstage hypnosis acts. For example, a hypnotized subject who's told that a piece of chalk is a burning cigarette will create a full-blown blister within 30 seconds of being touched by the cold chalk stick. The mind creates a physiologic "reality" that manifests the person's belief about the consequence of a burn, even though the chalk did not harm the skin.

Similarly, a hypnotized participant is asked to lift a glass of water, but is told that the glass weighs 1,000 pounds. The individual struggles, gets red in the face, sweats, and yet cannot budge the glass. By contracting the muscles used to lift the glass while contracting the muscles that put the glass down, the mind creates a behavioral "reality" that matches our belief that we cannot lift a half-ton glass. The net result is that the nervous system creates an isometric exercise in which the action of competing muscles expends tremendous energy, yet provides no net movement of the "heavy" glass.

If the mind truly controls our lives, as it does in the hypnosis examples previously cited, why doesn't it fulfill our conscious desires? The secret behind our problem is that we have failed to fully understand the nature and interaction between the two functionally different and interdependent subdivisions of the mind: the *subconscious* and *self-conscious* minds.

The *conscious mind,* the latest evolutionary modification of the nervous system, is centered in the *prefrontal cortex,* a lump of brain tissue just behind the forehead. The conscious mind is the seat of the personal identity that we associate with "self." It's the thinking, creative mind that contemplates and acts upon our wishes, desires, and aspirations.

In contrast, the *subconscious mind* is neither a thinking mind nor an especially creative mind. Its proficiency is that it's an unimaginably powerful record-playback mechanism. It downloads and stores stimulus-response behavioral programs acquired from instincts and life experiences. Upon perceiving an environmental signal, the subconscious reflexively activates previously stored behavioral responses—no thinking required.

An amazing characteristic of the conscious mind is that it isn't bound by time. Its thought-processing mechanism allows us to relive past experiences, leap into visions of the future, and even disconnect from the present moment as we contemplate "deep thoughts." In contrast, the activities of the subconscious mind are always fixed in the present moment; it doesn't readily discern a past or future. The conscious mind is free to time travel, because the programmable subconscious "autopilot" can navigate our vehicular bodies without the observation or awareness of the conscious mind.

When we control our behavior with the conscious mind, our hands are on the wheel, and we are in control of our life experiences. However, when the conscious mind is engaged in thought, or time traveling, by default behavior is controlled by the subconscious "autopilot." The conscious mind, not being observant at these moments, is generally unaware of the actions and consequences of our automated, preprogrammed subconscious behaviors.

Neuroscience reveals that our conscious minds are engaged in thought 95 percent or more of the time. This means that the conscious mind's wishes and desires only control our lives 5 percent of the time. Ninety-five percent of our lives are shaped by the decisions, actions, emotions, and behaviors of our subconscious programs.

The unobserved subconscious-autopilot mode represents the crux of the problem for why our lives don't match our conscious wishes and desires. Life problems generally arise from the fact that subconscious programs are beliefs and behaviors derived from observing and downloading other people's behaviors. As such, they don't necessarily represent our wishes and desires.

A baby born into this world experiences a mental state similar to a person with amnesia. *Who am I? What are my behaviors? What are my emotional traits?* The only way the child would learn the answers to these questions is through observation and feedback from other people surrounding him or her.

During the first six years of life, the child's brain unconsciously acquires the behavioral repertoire needed for him or her to become a functional member of society. Nature facilitates this learning experience by programming the child's brain activity to predominantly operate in the *theta* electroencephalogram (EEG) frequency (4 to 8 hertz), a neurologic state expressed as a hypnotic "trance." Children simply observe the behavioral patterns of their parents, siblings, and peers, and directly download them as behavioral programs into their own subconscious minds.

Parents also serve as the "mirror" that we use in defining who we are as individuals. While we are in the hypnogogic state, parental remarks that describe our personal traits and characteristics—such as our abilities, disabilities, worthiness, deservedness, and goodness or badness—are directly downloaded as beliefs that shape the character of our lives.

Psychologists recognize that up to 70 percent of these downloaded beliefs create negative, disempowering, and self-sabotaging behaviors. On those occasions when we observe ourselves engaging in self-destructive unconscious behaviors, we frequently attempt to control these subconscious programs by "talking" to ourselves. These efforts usually fail, leaving us frustrated and disheartened. The problem is that there's no entity in our subconscious minds to respond to our requests and coaching.

The good news is that our limiting subconscious programs are not fixed, immutable behaviors. After the age of six, we have the ability to rewrite disempowering beliefs and gain control over our lives by using repetitive, habit-creating behaviors. Hence, we need to engage in specific "practices" to acquire new subconscious programs and rewrite self-destructive habits.

Toward this end, we are offered the gift of an eminently simple and powerful reprogramming technique, the *See Feel Hear Challenge,* presented by Dr. Darren Weissman and Cate Montana. This process represents a valuable tool that supports the rewriting of our limiting subconscious beliefs and the creation of new habits. The See Feel Hear Challenge is a "pattern interrupt" process that empowers us to stop a negative pattern and choose an intentional, desired behavior. Through repetition, this process can facilitate the transformation of negative emotional patterns into authentic win-win opportunities.

The Heart of the Matter: A Simple Guide to Discovering Gifts in Strange Wrapping Paper represents both a wealth of information and an experiential work that offers guidance and tactics for rewriting the limiting, self-sabotaging perceptions that we inevitably acquire during the first six years of our lives. Knowledge is power, and the awareness of "self" provided in the See Feel Hear Challenge is knowledge that can manifest personal self-empowerment.

By learning and using Darren's process for digesting and healing developmental emotional wounds, the See Feel Hear Challenge is a life-enhancing strategy that can help us lovingly transform our world and fulfill our most creative and powerful selves.

Bruce H. Lipton, Ph.D.,
cell biologist, best-selling author of
The Biology of Belief and *The Honeymoon Effect,*
and co-author of *Spontaneous Evolution*

Preface by
Dr. Darren Weissman

This Is a Journey of Love

The Western Wall surrounding the ancient Temple Mount in the Old City of Jerusalem is a sacred site that has drawn pilgrimages and prayers for hundreds of years. Built by Herod the Great around 19 B.C.E., the site has long been known as the "the Place of Weeping," where men and women offer their prayers on slips of paper, shoving them in the cracks of the wall between the stones. Over the centuries, millions of pieces of paper have been stuffed between the stones of the Wailing Wall, talismans of billions of tears and heartrending human experiences.

I made my own pilgrimage to the Wailing Wall in January 2004, when I traveled to Israel to conduct a Life-Line seminar. It was a deeply meaningful moment for me, being a member of the Jewish faith, as I approached this most sacred of sites with my wife, Sarit. It was a novel experience for her, with no formal religious background whatsoever, to be surrounded by modern-day pilgrims, all fervently intent on bringing their hopes and troubles to a place where they might offer them up to God for resolution.

As I made my way toward the men's side of the wall, I lost sight of her amid the throng of tourists, shawled women, and bearded men in their black coats and hats. Intent in my own moment, and content with Sarit having her own experience, I didn't see her walk up to the wall and hesitate a foot away from it. I didn't see her suddenly burst into tears and cover her face with her hands, nor did I see her step away from the wall in wonder, as the sun instantly dried the tears on her face.

"I don't know what it was," she said later, still visibly shaken. "When I got close to the wall, I couldn't keep from crying. It was like an electrical charge that I couldn't escape. I didn't stop crying until I walked away to come meet you."

Fresh from my own encounter, I knew exactly what she'd tapped into. Both of us had entered an emotionally charged field, saturated with thousands of years of suffering, fear, and hatred—the weeping of women for their husbands who died in battle, the agonizing tears shed over dead and dying children, the rage-filled tears of men who had lost wives and comrades—all psychically encased in stone and crumbling cement.

What's Your Wailing Wall?

The Wailing Wall isn't the only place where emotion accumulates. We all have our emotional wailing walls. We carry ourselves around in them all day long, and express and identify through them every day.

Yes, over time our bodies can become "the Place of Weeping." Our emotions and the associated memories get buried in the matter of our bones and stay there, misunderstood and ignored. As a result, they damage us, hurt others, and impact the world around us. If we're incapable of handling these emotions, over time they become toxic, affecting us physically and mentally, and erupting into all sorts of symptoms that we experience as unhappiness, depression, and disease.

We can all relate. No one is exempt! The result? Our society has become one massive Wailing Wall. All it takes is an honest look at the world around us to really get how much humanity is genuinely suffering. And these conditions are perpetuated each and every day.

The Heart of the Matter

Let's play a little game. Just for a minute, imagine that you're a humanoid from another galactic world called Harmonia. You've packed the wife and kids into your interstellar cruiser to go on an extended vacation, looking for fun places to visit. Along the way, you see a planet, all blue, green, white, and brown, sparkling like a jewel in a solar system on the edge of the Milky Way galaxy. You hold a family meeting and decide, "Wow, what a gorgeous planet! What a great place to let the kids stretch their legs and mingle with an alien culture for a few years! Let's check it out!"

You learn the lingo and dress codes, and then beam down and start talking to a bunch of people in a country called the United States. The people are really friendly, and you like them a lot. But you also discover that . . .

❤ . . . 56 percent of 10- to 14-year-old girls engage in self-mutilation.[1]

❤ . . . 26 percent of the population suffers from a diagnosable mental-health disorder.[2]

❤ . . . 11 percent of people aged 12 years and over take antidepressant medication.[3]

- ❦ . . . 1 out of 2 Americans has at least one chronic disease,[4] and 1 out of 3 is obese.

- ❦ . . . diagnosis of children with chronic illnesses such as asthma, obesity, and ADD has quadrupled in one generation.[5]

- ❦ . . . 41 to 50 percent of all first marriages end in divorce.[6]

- ❦ . . . suicide was the 10th leading cause of death in 2010.[7]

Would you want to hang around? Would you let your precious children live in such a place, even for a short period of time? Of course not! You'd hop back into your spacecraft, reset the GPS (Galactic Positioning System), and hightail it out of here!

The See Feel Hear Challenge

Leaving Earth and what we believe to be our self-created troubles behind is not an option. It's time to deal with them and their unseen, unrecognized, unprocessed emotional core. That's why we've written *The Heart of the Matter: A Simple Guide to Discovering Gifts in Strange Wrapping Paper.* As a holistic physician and the developer of The LifeLine Technique®, I have come to understand, in

19 years of healing work, that every physical symptom and stressful situation in life represents reactive emotional patterns stemming from the subconscious mind. Accessing and assimilating these hidden emotional patterns that run our lives is the most important job of everyone on our planet today. Unless we understand and harness the power of our emotions to work for us instead of against us, we'll never learn to live at the level of joyous creation and cooperation.

Unlike the family from Harmonia, most people don't get how critical the situation is. Every day, we see and hear the kinds of statistics in the previous list. But we don't feel the truth of them anymore. We don't see, feel, or hear the inner messages and truths our own bodies are sending us every day. We don't pay attention to our hearts' desires and the still, small voice within that speaks to us of our dreams and longings and our need for change. If we did pay attention to these things, we'd be happier people, and the cumulative effect on our culture would be an experience that we have yet to discover: peace, love, and inspiration.

The simple yet potent technique taught in this book, called the See Feel Hear Challenge, is designed to help you access and assimilate hidden emotional patterns that run your life so that you can harness the power of your emotions to work for you instead of against you. It's an "in the trenches" tool you can use to transform perceived negative emotional patterns into an authentic dialogue so that you can evolve into the person you've always longed to be—and are truly destined to be. By learning and using the See Feel Hear Challenge, you'll find the consequences of the emotional patterns held in your body and mind naturally fading away. You'll be able to make positive decisions and changes for yourself. This, in turn, will positively influence your personal relationships with your family members, friends, co-workers, and the world you're a part of.

Is it easy? Actually, yes. But first you must stand in front of your personal Wailing Wall, acknowledge your feelings, and, as Sarit did in the Old City of Jerusalem that day, face them. When you do, you'll discover that there's nothing to be afraid of. You'll discover that, like all of the little notes stuffed into the wall, the pain and symptoms in our minds and hearts, our bodies, our relationships, and our world are messages to ourselves—gifts in strange wrapping paper—that, once seen, felt, and heard, will liberate us to experience a whole new and conscious way of living.

With Infinite Love & Gratitude,
Darren

PREFACE BY
CATE MONTANA

I first met Darren while working with the creators of the movie *What the Bleep Do We Know!?* As editor of the movie's online newsletter, *The Bleeping Herald,* I wrote a review of Darren's book *The Power of Infinite Love & Gratitude* in May 2006. I even recall the quote I used to start the review:

> A single moment truly lived is the same as living a thousand lifetimes. The wisdom of the universe teaches us that each moment is genuinely experienced when we awaken to the power of Infinite Love & Gratitude—the key to mastering the game of life.

I was deeply impressed by the book and equally impressed when I met Darren in person later that year. During an afternoon appointment, he did a LifeLine Technique session with me, and then a bunch of us went out for dinner at an Indian restaurant. His passion for healing, incredible expertise, caring heart, and blessed straightforwardness and enthusiasm for life were both refreshing and inspiring.

When I started an online newspaper called *The Global Intelligencer,* Darren was my first pick to write the health column. I was thrilled when he agreed, and thus followed a great working and writing relationship that lasted until I dissolved the publication. When I learned about *The Heart of the Matter,* I was immediately drawn to the project. I'd just finished writing two books. One was a social commentary called *GhettoPhysics,* with Will Arntz and Eray Brown. The other was a very intense memoir about awakening to my inner feminine essence after a 40-year sleep during which I dreamed that the safest and most productive way to express myself on this planet was to camouflage my female sensitivities and operate as "just one of the guys."

To accomplish this, I cultivated a tough, competitive, intellectual, smart-mouthed attitude about life. But there was a terrible price to pay for adopting this imbalanced, masculinized persona. I had to cauterize my feelings and emotions. I had to put myself ahead of others. I had to constantly compete to ensure success. All of this was to serve one goal: obtaining the insubstantial security of success and money.

Unfortunately, what got left behind in the process— what's being left behind more and more in people's lives nowadays—was my heart and that "single moment truly lived" that Darren talked about in his first book. It took a decade of deep introspection and a conscious peeling away of the protective barriers to feeling vulnerability, love, and caring to revive my feminine soul, and then another year spent writing about the journey to get back on track as a whole and responsive human being. Participating as co-author of a heart-based book designed to help people recover their own emotional and spiritual compass was the perfect next step in my own awakening.

A Lesson in Genuineness

Being present to love and appreciation for life, being real and available with self and others, is the heart of the matter. And don't you know that Darren slam-dunked me straight into it during our very first conference call, giving me a firsthand experience of how powerful the See Feel Hear Challenge really is.

I was under deadline to finish a book proposal, doing rewrites of the screenplay *Zentropy* for Hollywood producer Betsy Chasse and helping a close friend pack up her life to move to India. Between working, taking stuff to Goodwill, and helping my friend repaint her house so that she wouldn't get dinged for the damage deposit, I was woefully unprepared for Darren's call. Even though we'd worked together before, I was nervous and unsure. I wanted to look good! Did Darren support my little insecurity dance? No way!

Compellingly heartfelt with me, he was utterly present during our conversation, with no agendas or expectations. The result? I couldn't help but rise to his higher frequency of interpersonal engagement. I blurted out the truth of how unprepared I was, confessed to the stress I was feeling, and admitted wanting to look good going into the project and how I feared I wouldn't.

On the spot he led me through the See Feel Hear Challenge to connect and transform the subconscious patterns that were driving the painful emotions I was experiencing. Twenty-three minutes later, after I plummeted briefly and painlessly down what he terms a "black hole" of core potential surrounding insecurity and trust, I popped out the other side into the realness of present-time consciousness, better known as "the now."

"So, how do you feel?" he asked me quietly.

All the anxiety and upset had vanished, as well as the negative self-talk in my head. I felt clear and present. The huge fir tree in the corner of my backyard, the blossoming tulips, the swiftly overgrowing spring grasses—I was consciously linked to all of them, just as I was obviously consciously linked to Darren in a living dance that far transcended silly personality and image concerns. I told him what I was experiencing.

"Welcome to present-time consciousness," he said.

It's been a tremendous honor to be part of this book and Darren's work. It's been a blessing to learn the See Feel Hear Challenge, and as life has had its tumultuous way with me these past months, it's been an even greater blessing to be able to *use* the process. Over and over I've addressed troubles and worries and emotional storms, big and small, as they've shown up. And boy, have they shown up!

The bottom line is, this process works. It's simple, and you can do it in a matter of minutes; it's profound, and you can use it to dig deep. I am a different, happier, and a more emotionally centered person for using it. As a newbie on Darren's Infinite Love & Gratitude team, I've only got one piece of advice: after you've read this book, please use the information! You've got to use the See Feel Hear Challenge for it to do any good.

So without further ado, welcome to *The Heart of the Matter*. Welcome to the process that will lead you to that "single moment truly lived," the moment that already contains everything, the pearl of great price, compared to which all the trappings of modern society's idea of happiness fade to insignificance.

With Infinite Love & Gratitude,
Cate

INTRODUCTION

Change is a journey of love—and guts, gumption, tears, toil, and tremendous joy. You've got to love yourself to want to take the journey. You've got to love yourself to pick up the evolutionary tools and actually use them to do the work of transformation. And you've got to be responsible if you're the one building the tools and putting a book like *The Heart of the Matter* out into the marketplace.

Early in the creation process, Darren and I were discussing the Prefaces, and he said, "This book is a journey of love." The words grabbed me, and I promptly deleted whatever phrase originally opened his Preface, stuck that sentence in there, and read it back to him.

"That's it!" he said.

But then we had to sit and ask ourselves, "Well, that's nice. But what is love in this context? How does it show up?" As we talked, we realized that every aspect of the project was part of the journey of love, from Darren's original intent to bring a healing process into the world that regular people could use—from librarians to chicken farmers to CEOs of global corporations—to ensuring that every word, example, and quote in the book emanated the highest level of consciousness possible to making sure that *we* resonated to the highest possible level of consciousness every time we talked, wrote, edited, or sweated over formatting the endnotes.

Along the way, we rediscovered that love isn't limited to any given thing, not even an emotion. It's a process that translates the intent of the intangible ideal of "love" into tangible, concrete expressions that can be experienced and shared, uplifting everything and everyone along the way.

Such is the power of love in action!

This is, of course, how Darren's whole career as a holistic physician and healing pioneer can be described. For almost 20 years, he's been the catalyst of love in action, successfully assisting thousands of clients in their healing journeys. Since the mystical "download" he experienced in June 2002—a spontaneous blessing where he awakened to a completely new way of viewing bodily symptoms, stress in relationships, and the power to manifest with intention—he's rigorously designed, expanded, used, and taught The LifeLine Technique, a process capable of awakening new perceptions, bridging the gap between the conscious and subconscious, and activating the body's natural potential for healing. Darren has conducted seminars, taught the LifeLine Technique all around the world, and written two books titled *The Power of Infinite Love & Gratitude* and *Awakening to the Secret Code of Your Mind.*

Despite all his work, Darren felt an immense desire to help even more people who are suffering in the world. "There was this pulling in my heart that kept me open to other possibilities, new ways of getting the benefits of The LifeLine Technique out to people," he said.

After several years, he hit upon the See Feel Hear Challenge, the simple, do-it-yourself transformational technique taught in this book. A powerful process that Darren extrapolated from a portal in the 16-step LifeLine Technique called the Person, Place, Memory, and Addiction Portal, the See Feel Hear Challenge is designed to help you learn, heal, grow, and evolve by processing emotions that correlate with stressful people, places, memories, and addictions via visual, kinesthetic, and auditory pathways of the brain and body. "People who are suffering with chronic pain, emotional overload, and self-destructive thoughts and behaviors were all finding relief by applying this portion of The LifeLine Technique to their lives," Darren said. "It suddenly hit me that this was the perfect stand-alone process I'd been looking for all along."

As we worked on the book, it became evident that our "love in action" journey was greater than the See Feel Hear Challenge itself or the frequency of the words we used to describe it. Our collaboration itself was part of the "new way," part of the paradigm of the New World that so many people dream of establishing. "I knew in my heart that it was vital to find someone to help me communicate the See Feel Hear Challenge process and its use in crystal clear terms," said Darren. "I hadn't connected with Cate in over a year, and wouldn't you know, she 'coincidentally' contacted me just as I was starting the book. Her extensive background as a journalist, her scientific knowledge from her years of working with the filmmakers of *What the Bleep Do We Know!?*, our previous working relationship, and her conscious journey of self-discovery made her the perfect fit as a writer."

But why put some unknown journalist's name on the cover as co-author? Darren was the expert, the physician, the teacher, and an author in his own right. Why not just pay me to help with the writing process and be done with it?

Because that's not the way love chose to show up.

With love as Darren's stated intent for the book, the need for ownership of ideas was eradicated. Any need to be the "top dog" or "the expert" or "the author" disappeared. His instantaneous, absolute, and humble acceptance of me as a full-on partner in the project astounded me! But then part of what we learned while writing *The Heart of the Matter* is that much of the mystery of love is that it makes things greater. When other elements and people that match the frequency of the intent are invited to join the show as equal partners, the sum of the whole becomes greater than that of its parts. It's the whole "Wherever two or more are gathered in My (Love's) name, there I am" routine.

"It's been amazing," says Darren. "Yes, the See Feel Hear Challenge is part of my vision and a process of the LifeLine. But *The Heart of the Matter* is what it is because of Cate's word craft and the mastery of her amazing soul. We came together as equals from disparate backgrounds to write this book, and the end result is far beyond what just one person could accomplish."

The bottom line is that the collaboration became a talisman to the technique that we were communicating. We refused to let anything stand in the way of coming from the heart and communicating heart values. We used the See Feel Hear Challenge extensively to deal with whatever came up, both individually and with one another. The result? Writing the book was fun and almost effortless, and the richly dynamic content that came forward excited us both.

A Final Note Before We Begin

Outside of the Prefaces and this Introduction, there is only "one voice" throughout *The Heart of the Matter* that comes from both of us as an individual unit. In the rare cases where the use of the word *I* does creep in, it's always Darren speaking from his personal experience as the developer, teacher, and facilitator of The LifeLine Technique and the See Feel Hear Challenge, and you'll notice that this occurs in boxed text throughout.

The book is straightforward and doesn't pull any punches as it explores human emotions and other essential, yet tricky, subjects: truth, perception, the subconscious mind, suffering and disease, core beliefs, and how all these things work together. The first four chapters cover the basics of all these subjects and introduce you to the See Feel Hear Challenge. Be prepared to jump in with pen and paper handy! As you learn the technique, there are tons of insightful processes that you can do as well as the Challenge itself. You will be amazed at what you discover about yourself, your dreams, and the contents of your subconscious!

The second part of the book explains why the See Feel Hear Challenge process works so effectively and rapidly, and the third part takes a brief look at various human dynamics that make change difficult, keeping us from living happy, purposeful lives. In the final part of the book, I put on my journalism hat, and Darren speaks for himself in two chapters of questions and answers designed to clarify and expand the use of the See Feel Hear Challenge process.

Now you know how the book came to be. May your journey into *The Heart of the Matter* be as fruitful as ours has been!

Part I

WHAT IS THE HEART OF THE MATTER?

Chapter 1

Learning Life's Curriculum

"From the clear center of my heart, there are no edges to my loving you. I've heard it said there's a window that opens from one mind to another; but if there were no wall, what need of installing a window?"

— R U M I [1]

Children live the way most of us want to: eyes shining, brimming with exuberance; the world is their oyster. No separation distorts their minds and hearts. They have no walls and thus no need for windows to peer into the soul of another person. In their uninhibited heart space,

3

there are no boundaries, hesitations, fears, or inner discussions about appropriateness; no "voices in the head" passing judgment about feelings and actions. The child loves absolutely, hates and despairs absolutely, and laughs absolutely all in the space of a few minutes, emotions flowing like a clean river from the core of his or her being.

Who can fail to respond to that? Love that? As adults, we watch our children and then look in the mirror and wonder, *When did I lose that breathless passion? How did my unthinking heart connection to everything and everyone fade? Where did the dancing eyes go?* We think, *Well, I was fine as a little kid, and then life happened! My parents got divorced. My fourth-grade teacher hated me. I was bullied by my classmates. My sister got all the attention. I was molested.* The litany of heartaches and grievances add up, all too quickly replacing the simple joy we were born into. Gradually we enter the place of separation, and the yearning begins.

What makes the difference between a happy, exuberant, fulfilling life and a nonproductive, halfhearted, anxious one? How is it possible to stay openhearted when so much of life is painful? How is it possible to go beyond stress and thrive? Great questions! And although it may seem overly simple, the best, most empowering answer is *choice.* Many of us live our lives by accident, stumbling into relationships; wandering into careers; searching for meaning; and hoping and praying we'll get lucky in love, find our fortune, and stay healthy. We never discover what living on purpose truly means. We transition from ebullient child to weary adult, never noticing the mileposts along the way, unaware of the myriad opportunities we have to stop, reflect, and choose differently—all because we're not taught to be aware and to know that we have a choice.

Purposeful living embraces self-knowledge, reason, and faith. Reason provides clear goals that spring from knowing our authentic selves, while faith and intuition teach us to trust the process of our lives. But if we're not taught how to find self-knowledge, if we don't understand how we get offtrack, if we don't know how to get clear in the first place, how do we find our path? Our lives and the world around us are filled with drama and difficulty, beauty and bizarreness, joys and sorrows. Life is an emotional adventure, and there's so much happening so fast! Situations and people can knock us off course. Arbitrary things seem to stand in the way of discovering and manifesting our vision. Our joy is so easily taken away.

Earth is a school, and our daily lives are classrooms in which we learn life lessons. But unless we grasp the nature of the school, the nature of ourselves as students, and the nature of the lessons we're supposed to learn, we're blind as bats in a cage. Purpose and happiness elude us! Without knowing exactly what we're dealing with and without the tools to manage our lives, we end up scared and miserable, repeating painful lessons over and over again, suffering from all sorts of disabilities and diseases. But given the right understanding and the right tools, we can soar through Earth School; get in touch with our hearts; and get on with creating the quality relationships, security, and health that are our natural birthright.

Doing the See Feel Hear Challenge has caused major shifts in my relationship with myself and others. By being able to see and observe my emotions without judgment, by experiencing the quality of what I feel instead of analyzing everything all the time, by listening to the voice of my emotions with the ear of my soul rather than my physical ear, I have been able to move forward and begin to develop self-love day by day. The See Feel Hear Challenge might sound like a simple challenge, but it's so expansive in its nature that there's no limit to it!

— Betty K.

Earth Reality and Perception

Because we live in a physical reality, our attention is generally monopolized by the stuff of everyday life: the challenges of getting an education; earning a living; and dealing with relationships, family, and health. Our dramas play out in the theater of gain and loss, desire and satisfaction, and they seem entirely real and important to us. We base our happiness upon events unfolding in alignment with our desires and expectations. In doing our best to make things work out the way we want them to, we often suffer from stress and anxiety. We become fixated on achieving our goals, and our entire persona— our view of who we are—becomes attached to the outcomes of our desires.

We're crushed when we don't get what we want. We get upset when we get what we don't want. When we get exactly what we do want, often it doesn't turn out to be as wonderful as we thought it would be. Even when we attain the pinnacle of our hearts' desires, the moment of attainment and the joy itself passes. It's simply the nature of the physical world and how things work. Eventually, maybe through a trauma, a death in the family, an injury, or some other adversity, we finally notice that physical reality, even at its best, leads to dissatisfaction.

Realizing this, we catch a glimpse of a more transcendent and satisfying reality: the big picture of oneness and interconnection that's waiting for us. We begin to long for things that are more meaningful, like inner peace and a happiness that isn't grounded in transitory situations and perishable items. We begin to search for understanding and meaning. We long to hear and feel at a greater depth. We want intimacy and authenticity with ourselves and in our relationships. We want healthy bodies, flexible minds, and inner fulfillment.

It's at this point that we bump up against all the learned self-beliefs that we think are holding us back from attaining these things. The result of life experiences starting the day we were born (and even in utero), these "core beliefs," whether they're positive or negative, end up running the show. If we've learned to believe that we are intelligent go-getters—that's how we think and behave. If we've gathered experiences that push us into low self-esteem and confusion, that's how we express ourselves. Whether it's beliefs about God, the value of a good education, the vital importance of flossing, or a blind faith in doctors, by early adulthood core beliefs are the invisible traffic cops directing our lives. Encoded in the circuitry of our memory networks, they even determine the expression of our genetic potential for both health and disease.

Experiencing joy, authenticity, and purpose in life begins when we start the process of discovering our personal truths. And we do this by examining and shifting untrue or negative core beliefs that eclipse our true selves. Unfortunately, we fiercely believe the things we've come to believe! "Hey, no pain no gain," says the athlete who's wrapping her swollen knee before heading out on the jogging trail. "Why be a man when you can be a success?" comments the workaholic as he laughs and gets into his BMW at midnight to go home.

Limiting core beliefs cripple our ability to be authentic and respond to the reality of circumstances from our deepest personal truths. If left alone, limiting core beliefs set degenerative patterns into motion on mental, emotional, biochemical, structural, and spiritual levels, ultimately keeping us from loving, being loved, trusting, or being trusted. We begin to think, feel, speak, and act in ever more limited ways. And the cells of our bodies mirror these perceived limitations, feeding the identity of the limiting belief. It becomes extremely difficult to experience joy and fulfillment, and inevitably the body begins to decline.

Usually not until we have a breakdown of some sort do we take the time to question the value of what's driving us. But even here, we run into the catch-22 of core beliefs. The athlete with the swollen knee keeps pushing herself until she ends up with bursitis. She believes that the body is fundamentally a machine and that diseases are "accidents that happen" to machines. So she takes cortisone shots and keeps running.

But if she would stop to contemplate her body and the pain, and let them talk to her—if she'd look for a deeper truth within her situation—she'd find that there was an important message from her true self waiting in the in-box of her subconscious. And the message would say, "Hey,

9

stop! Smell the roses, darling! I'm not a machine! I'm life! And I'm talking to you with this inflammation, doing my best to get your attention so that you don't run us both into the ground with this self-destructive core belief of 'no pain, no gain'"!

Gifts in Strange Wrapping Paper

Aches and pains, diseases, and emotional suffering are not simply "bad things that happen to good people." That's a core belief that has to go. Suffering and disease, unhappiness and anxiety, depression and anger are not just happenstances. They're gifts in strange wrapping paper, messages stuffed into our subconscious Wailing Walls that haven't been read, messages speaking to us through the communication channels available: our bodies and our relationships.

Learning how to read these messages, we discover the truth of who we are. We discover what our purpose is. We learn how to see life, our bodies, and suffering differently. We open our hearts and senses to feel what's going on beneath the surface of things; we develop our psychic senses and become sensitive in the finest sense of the word, open to our innermost truths. We hear more acutely the whispers of the infinite love and potential that lie within us, outshouted by society's core belief that to live well, we must consume and run and run and run.

Unfortunately, most people in Earth School experiencing so-called illnesses have not been taught to see symptoms as messages. They have no clue that symptoms are pointing toward a hidden treasure of subconscious emotions that, once revealed, can liberate them to experience the lives they've always dreamed of. And so instead of addressing the inner emotional connection to disease, they focus only on the physical symptoms and suffer hugely as a result.

In Earth School things are often not what they seem. Like disease, emotions don't happen by accident. They, too, are messengers from the subconscious mind. Literally the energy of creation in motion, *e-motions* can be felt, exchanged, and measured over distance and have an incredible impact upon our bodies. Every thought we think bears an emotional charge that can alter body chemistry and heart and brain rhythms. Depending upon the frequency signature of the e-motion, emotional effects can range from highly positive and transformative to highly destructive. If unresolved, suppressed, and left misunderstood, emotions can wreak all sorts of havoc, forming the roots of suffering.

Understanding the emotional root of "dis-ease" in no way implies that medical intervention is bad, wrong, or inappropriate. That would be completely counterproductive, ignoring the amazing advances of science and symptom-based care. In reality, this discovery provides a bridge to the deeper emotional component that Western medicine has so far been unable to link into the healing process.

Darren's Astounding Discovery

What I've discovered from doing well over 100,000 LifeLine sessions is that regardless of the stressful conditions we experience, regardless of external contributing factors such as toxins, pollution, poor diet, and so on, *every disease has a subconscious emotional root.* Allergies, infection, stomach pain, addiction, depression, injuries such as stubbing your toe in the middle of the night, twisting your ankle while jogging—these aren't consciously manifested experiences, but rather subconsciously triggered manifestations of emotions revealing themselves in uniquely appropriate ways.

Subconscious emotional patterns influence the way we think, feel, speak, and behave, both physically and psychologically. When activated, they influence our minds and bodies, setting into motion events that take us out of the present moment like flashes of lightning, creating thunderous rumbles in all parts of our human experience.

I know it may seem strange, or even outrageous, to state that all symptoms, stress, and disease stem from undigested subconscious emotions. However, when we begin to understand the mind, specifically the subconscious, we learn that these symptoms are not personal in any way, but rather spiritual in every way: they are wake-up calls to alert us to evolve to our fullest potential.

Love is the foundation of creation, and every emotion, even hate, is a permutation of love. As we learn how to understand and process the emotional patterns stored in our subconscious minds, we awaken our authentic nature to live in the moment. Gradually, we become more like the healthy, joyous children we were created to be.

Any day we desire, we can commit ourselves to starting this change. Any day we desire—next year, next month, next week, tomorrow, or right now—we can free our hearts and minds to a new way of being in the world; we can embrace the process of change. Everything we need to experience, all our dreams and desires, is present within us right now. By understanding a few Earth School basics, emptying the trash, and cleaning out a few closets, we begin the journey of knowing our soul's deepest truth.

❤

Chapter 2

Hell No!

"Learn the alchemy true human beings know:
The moment you accept what troubles you've
been given, the door will open."

— RUMI[1]

It's hard to talk about "the truth." Not because it doesn't exist, but rather because there's rarely much consensus about it. It's hard to imagine a hundred people answering a question in exactly the same way, let alone everyone on the planet. Differences in age, gender, race, religion, nationality, and political preference have historically stood in the way of people's ability to get along and agree. That said, there is actually one question, the "truth question," that every person on the planet answers almost identically.

Sound impossible? Let's go for a test drive. Take a moment to observe your body. Is it talking to you with headaches or allergies? Do you experience chronic pain, acne, poor eyesight, infertility, or asthma? How about digestive challenges, high blood pressure, constipation, obesity, hormone imbalances, or chronic fatigue? Do you have debilitating physical symptoms or traumatic health concerns like cancer or diabetes?

Now take a moment to tune in to your personal life. How are your relationships? What are your responsibilities as a mom or dad, husband or wife, daughter or son, student, employee or employer? Do you feel stressed in any way? Are there stressful people and circumstances that come to mind? How's the money situation? Does your heart feel heavy? Do you ever feel unworthy, fearful, stuck, lonely, vulnerable, resentful, unsafe, or other painful kinds of emotion? Have you been labeled with depression, ADD, bipolar disorder, or PTSD?

Welcome to the human race! Everyone experiences many of these things to a greater or lesser degree. But now here comes the truth question: Would you ever choose to have any symptom or disease in your body or relationships? Given the opportunity to create your life, a day, or even a moment in time, would you choose to feel angry, depressed, fearful, or overwhelmed?

Every human being alive has the same answer: "Hell no!" Who in his or her right mind would ever choose to experience cancer, allergies, headaches, abuse, anxiety, betrayal, unworthiness, or any other painful condition? The truth question really could be called the "ridiculous question." However, we discover its incredible usefulness as soon as we ask the next logical question that comes to mind: If no one consciously chooses them and yet everybody experiences these things, why does this happen, and where do these painful, scary, and stressful circumstances come from?

The Subconscious Mind

If you aren't acting from conscious choice, something is triggering a reactive pattern in your mind and body that's causing you to express yourself with symptoms, stress, and disease. And the "something" driving these reactions is called the *subconscious mind.* What isn't an action is a reaction. And all reactions stem from the subconscious mind.

The subconscious mind is an energy and information field of pure potential, conducting the symphony of function and formation of everything ranging from the health of our bodies and relationships, to the personalities and personae that show up as "us" in different situations. It's a real behind-the-scenes coach, director, protector, and teacher, driving between 90 and 98 percent of what's happening. That's right. We're only conscious of what we do and why we do it between two and ten percent of the time!

The subconscious not only runs most of our lives on a moment-to-moment basis, but also conducts the function of the more than 50 trillion cells of our physical bodies. It's also the most amazing storage locker ever conceived. All our life experiences are stored in subconscious memory files alongside survival patterns, environmental imprints, belief systems, and conditioned emotional expressions. And the truly amazing thing is that we haven't got a clue that this mysterious and magical storage locker filled with memories and beliefs even exists until, like a submarine, it surfaces or shoots a torpedo!

Let's take a look at a guy called Sam and use him as an example of how the subconscious actually works in our lives. Right now Sam is 22 years young, but back when he was 2, he was sitting on the floor one night playing while his mother read a book. The summer evening was warm, and he was dressed in a long-sleeved, pale-blue top. The window was open, and the scent of honeysuckle filled the room. All of a sudden, a bat flew in the window. His mother grabbed Sam and ran out the door, screaming. Unfortunately, Sam's sleeve caught on the edge of the door strike, and his arm was almost jerked from its socket. Naturally, he started to scream and cry. At this point, his father ran to the rescue and killed the poor bat with a broom.

Fast-forward 20 years, and guess what? Sam has chronic shoulder pain. He works at a pest-control company and finds his job deeply rewarding. The only thing he doesn't like are the long-sleeved shirts the company insists that employees wear during the winter. On this particular day, Sam is excited, because after flirting for months, he finally has a date with the secretary in the office. He picks her up after work, and they head off to dinner. But even though the evening goes well, for some strange reason he suddenly finds her company mildly irritating. The date doesn't fulfill his expectations, and their romance never gets off the ground.

What has happened?

Unbeknownst to Sam, his date is wearing a new perfume that she bought especially for the evening called Honeysuckle Nights. That and her pale-blue dress trigger the parts of Sam's brain that subconsciously associate both the color and the scent with trauma. He doesn't realize this, of course—not any more than he is aware that he works as an exterminator because he subconsciously wants control in situations where, as a two-year-old, he had none; or that he loves his job because he associates getting rid of pests with being a hero, as his father had been that night.

And we think we call all the shots in our lives. Hardly! With the score at Subconscious 90 to 98 percent versus Conscious 2 to 10 percent, we haven't got a chance—not without some tools to help make the subconscious material understandable and meaningful when it does show up. And making subconscious emotional material known and available to us so that we can intentionally process it is what the See Feel Hear Challenge is all about.

Buried Treasure

We don't know what we don't know. And because of this, we are often easily derailed. The simple dynamics of living a healthy lifestyle, fighting an infection, and even going out on a date and maintaining healthy relationships become difficult and complicated due to our subconscious programs. But the subconscious mind is not our enemy. It's a diligent protector and a masterful teacher. And what do you say when someone protects you or teaches you something valuable? Exactly—you say, "Thank you!"

I had chronic pain in the ball of one foot, so I ran a See Feel Hear Challenge on it. It was only a faint symptom at the time, but as I tapped into the sensation, it was as if I'd struck oil! Emotions of anger came spewing to the surface, followed by a deep sadness and uncontrollable tears. I went through the whole process to fully digest the emotions that had been obviously accumulated and stored in the ball of my foot.

Afterward, I felt a deep clarity and calm similar to how it feels after a rainstorm, fresh and light. Since then, I have not experienced the pain again—and that was a few years ago!

— Janice R.

So how does the subconscious mind serve as a protector? Well, have you ever had the experience of "going elsewhere" or "tuning out" during an emotional storm? When situations are seemingly too traumatic and we don't have the tools, strategies, or support to consciously process what's going on, the subconscious mind compartmentalizes the incoming information, tucking it away for safekeeping. It buffers us from an overload of emotional input. Unless these traumatic emotions are eventually processed, we carry them around undigested in our subconscious minds for the rest of our lives. That's exactly what happened to our friend Sam that night with the bat. At age two he was unable to process and understand the commotion, pain, and fear he experienced. And his parents didn't have the conscious tools to help him process the emotions of the experience either. As a consequence, Sam's subconscious mind automatically created a protective cocoon around the circumstances, freezing all of the sensory experiences of the moment for later processing.

Although most psychologists agree that the majority of life circumstances that mold our personalities occur within the first five years of life, this buffering and stuffing away of emotions happens on an ongoing basis throughout our lives. Abuse and accidents, any highly charged situation where we feel overwhelmed, can add to our stockpile of buried emotions. Is it any wonder that we all have so much unaddressed subconscious material driving us?

The subconscious mind itself never chooses and never judges. It works in the background, associating all the stored information with ongoing moment-to-moment input. If we have an experience that triggers something in that storehouse of buried treasure, we react—just as Sam did to the scent of honeysuckle perfume that night. The subconscious also acts as a broadcasting signal, attracting like signals as a means to reveal those stores of inner information. In other words, scents and colors, sights and sounds, words and thoughts, tastes and textures related to incidents and emotions in our subconscious attract similar incidents and emotions to us in the world so that we can emotionally react and "get" that there's something inside that needs to be revealed.

This buried treasure triggers us again and again and again. Have you ever said or heard someone say this? "I just couldn't help myself. I wanted to be _____ (compassionate, kind, understanding, and so on), but something just came over me!" That's the subconscious mind hard at work.

In order for us to heal and evolve, it's imperative that we uncover the invisible patterns of the subconscious and decipher its language. And part of that process is learning not to judge, but rather how to discern from the heart how the subconscious information within us shows up in our bodies and lives. This can be more easily said than done, because the primary ways in which subconscious patterns make themselves known are through pain, fear, and stress. Over time, these emotionally reactive patterns build up, speaking to us through a diseased body, relationships, company, community, politics, and the world.

Can you say . . . *human drama?*

Martin Luther King, Jr., once said, "Men often hate each other because they fear each other; they fear each other because they don't know each other; they don't know each other because they cannot communicate; they cannot communicate because they are separated." When it comes to the subconscious, the same thing applies. We hate unhappiness, stress, and disease because we're afraid of these things; we're afraid of them because we don't know that they are a *form of communication.* And finally, we don't acknowledge symptoms, stress, and disease as a form of communication, because we so desperately want to distance ourselves and run away to a better place, where they don't exist. But in creating this separation, we unwittingly avoid the lessons and opportunities these things hold for us.

We keep our buried treasures at bay.

Nothing happens "by accident," and treating difficult events and disease as if they were alien incursions from outside us just makes us victims. Distancing ourselves from these experiences and the emotions they evoke just creates more struggle—and more of the same experiences! This is why the truth question is so important. Knowing that no one ever consciously chooses unhappiness, stressors, or illness—even though we all experience these things—is a big neon sign saying, "Wake up. There's a reason for this, and the reason is inside you, waiting to be acknowledged, courageously embraced, and lived intentionally."

Isn't that a bitch? The causes behind all our perceived pain and problems lie *inside,* where we can actually do something about them. We're responsible. Ouch!

Response-Ability

Like a lot of people, maybe you have a core belief that whispers, "Responsibility is an onerous thing to be avoided." Maybe you feel an emotional reaction to the word? If so, perhaps it might help to look at it a different way. *Responsible* doesn't mean liable. It means *capable of response.*

Who wouldn't want that? If we're capable of responding authentically to life instead of blindly reacting, flailing around in a sea of subconsciously driven emotions as if we were still innocent two-year-olds, we can get on with purposeful living. We can get on with creating fulfilling lives that are no longer sabotaged by old programs. We can bridge the gap of separation between the subconscious and conscious minds, learning to recognize portals of possibilities where we once only saw problems.

Yes, the truth question lands us with responsibility. But using it also shifts judgment into discernment. Instead of reacting to difficult circumstances in our lives, we, in employing the truth question, are empowered to dig deep to find the root causes of unhappiness and lack of health. Rather than having us react to reactions, fear fear, or act "tough," protecting a part of ourselves that's already in a protective state, the truth question wakes us up to being present in the moment so that we can begin to acknowledge the heart of the matter: that we are spirits of pure love, and that symptoms, stress, and disease, on any level, represent an intelligent conversation rather than brokenness. Knowing that the subconscious doesn't choose or judge—that it just reacts—helps us begin the necessary step of entering our heart space so that we can begin the journey of conscious creation.

Can You Handle the Truth?

Take stock of your life: your health, your relationships, your finances, your day-to-day emotional state. Is everything absolutely to your satisfaction? Be honest!

Are you less than flexible in mind and body? Are there things you really want to do but find yourself avoiding? Do you feel somehow dissatisfied with life? With yourself? Are other people triggering emotional and mental distress? Are you suffering physical symptoms of disease?

Take your time and examine your life.

Make a list of the symptoms and stressors that come to mind. Remember, there's nothing bad or wrong about any of these things. The only question is, do you want to continue experiencing them?

Once you have your list, ask yourself the truth question for each item: "Would I ever consciously choose this? Given the opportunity to create my life, a day, or even a moment in time, would I choose to experience this?"

Just be with whatever comes up for you. Open yourself to the possibility that everything on your list is changeable, that there are steps you can take to shift all of it, that every item is a buried treasure from your subconscious—a messenger revealing a doorway toward a whole new way of life.

❦

Chapter 3

Hell Yes!

"A strong intention can make 'two oceans wide'
be the size of a blanket, or 'seven hundred years'
the time it takes to walk to someone you love."

— RUMI[1]

Life is intentional 100 percent of the time—which is quite a statement to make, considering that over 90 percent of what we are and do results from subconscious programs and motivations! How can life be 100 percent intentional if, most the time, we don't know why we're experiencing the things we experience?

The answer is that although life is intentional, we are not necessarily intentional. There's a larger blueprint to events, a mysterious pattern to evolution that human beings normally aren't privy to. We may not like or enjoy some of the "growing experiences" that our subconscious minds set us up with, but if we could grasp the bigger picture, we would see the mysterious patterns revealing their interconnected truth. We would know that we are always 100 percent on target and that we are where we need to be 100 percent of the time.

This is a pretty tough pill to swallow sometimes.

Staying open to life's intentional mystery and trusting it enough to roll with the punches is a developed art. And one of the greatest challenges to developing such trust lies in the core belief that we know so much. The truth is, we don't even know what we don't know! But instead of acknowledging this, we cling to the ridiculous notion that we're in charge. Our beliefs about the world and how things should be become the "be-all and end-all" for us. We become fixed in our judgments of what's good and bad, helpful and detrimental. And then when "life happens," we're knocked for a loop. We react in fearful ways and get caught up in cycles of pain, stress, and illness.

Of course, fear and pain reactions can sometimes be good things. Protective in nature, pain and fear are mechanisms for getting us out of danger's path, shoving us into gear to effect rapid and decisive change. Sustainable evolution is not built upon fear and protection,

however; it's based upon love and willingness to grow. The key to shifting a protective or pain-filled orientation is to remember the truth question: "Given a choice, would I consciously choose this or that?" And the answer, "Hell no!" is our acknowledgment that we would never choose the symptom, stressor, or disease in the first place.

> After having a stupid argument with my significant other over the dishes, I stayed connected to the anger and frustration that I was feeling, and I decided to do the See Feel Hear Challenge. I welcomed the emotions into my heart with love and gratitude, and then saw, felt, and heard them. By the end I could see the bigger picture, and I realized that the whole issue was a reaction to receiving unwanted advice. I asked myself the truth question: "Would I ever consciously choose to feel angry, frustrated, and insulted?" Of course, my answer was a big fat *no.* Then I asked myself, "When receiving unwanted advice, how would I like to be?" I realized that I would like to be open and receptive to the information, confident and secure enough in my abilities and methods of doing things to listen with an open heart and then move on. This became my intention, and since then, the See Feel Hear Challenge

has helped me to transform this ongoing painful emotional thorn in my side into an open flow of communication and clarity.

— Cindy P.

Asking the truth question is love in action, the first step in *response-ability* toward creating what we desire in our relationships, our health, and everything else in our lives. The next step is setting our intentions.

Setting Intentions

Everything is possible in an infinite universe. But there's a flip side to this that also says that nothing's for sure. Too many variables affect the big picture from moment to moment. Our thoughts and emotions constantly shift, triggering an endless variety of potentials that sometimes even cancel each other out. Setting an intention is a way to follow your passions, regardless of who or what you've subconsciously attracted into your life. The process acknowledges where you are, where you've been, and where you intend to be, emulating the magnificent creative power of the ever-evolving universal intelligence within us that is constantly striving to know itself in new and empowering ways.

Manifesting an intention requires more than simply thinking positively, saying positive words, and putting up pictures of what you want on a dream board. Those are wonderful things to do. But intention is all about tapping into your heart's desires, and effective change requires the power of e-motion to manifest the infinite possibilities that lie within us.

There are two golden rules for manifesting, and following them makes the difference between revolution and evolution in your life. Sure, sometimes we get impatient and want a revolution to shake things up. But *revolution* literally means to stay in one place while turning 360 degrees, ending up in exactly the same place where you started! Sound familiar? Who hasn't experienced a whirlwind of exterior change—a new job, a new lover, a new apartment, or all of the above—only to discover that nothing really changed at all? The same dramas were still happening, just in a different location and with different people.

In contrast to revolution, *evolution* is a gradual development in which something changes into a different, often more complex, and better form. In human beings, evolution happens in two ways: 1) it involves natural physical and psychological growth that follows life's transformational blueprint, and 2) it's created by conscious intent. So, what do you intend? What do you want to change now that the truth question has revealed that there are things in your life that you are ready, willing, and able to change? You know your "Hell No!" Now what's your "Hell Yes!"?

The Two Golden Rules of Manifesting an Intention

1. Focus on where you desire to go rather than what you want to go away. Setting an intention requires you to enter your heart space, to go beyond the pain and the perceived broken pieces of your life to that creative place in your heart. This is where the spark of the Divine lives within us all. It's from this space that we listen inwardly to what our hearts are urging us to embrace. Take your time as you open yourself up to the unique message and the way in which your heart is speaking to you. What is your heart's desire? Your heart's intention may make itself known via a feeling, a voice, or an image that you can translate into a word, such as *love, joy,* or *confidence.* Your heart knows your truth. Go for your "Hell Yes!"

2. Once you know your heart's desire, now it's time to focus on it as if you were already there. Become it. The brain and body don't know the differences among reality, memory, and imagination. Focus on your heart's desire as if you were already experiencing it. If your heart's desire is to know love or joy, then state it in the following way: "I am love" or "I am joy." This "I am" phrasing acknowledges the oneness and interconnectedness of the Universe that automatically activates the power of your subconscious mind.

The truth question and setting intentions aim straight to the heart of empowering you to create your life in alignment with your true self. They form the foundation of the See Feel Hear Challenge process that will be detailed in the next chapter. But before we move on to the process itself, there's one more tool that you need to pack in your evolutionary tool kit: your imagination!

Everything that exists is born from imagination. It is the alchemical key to turn a scribble into a masterpiece, a few notes into a ballad, and a fleeting thought into a vibrant reality. Taking the time to imagine your intention as a child imagines being a doctor, a fireman, or a ballerina gives you the e-motional feel of your intent. And once you can feel the emotion of your intention, you have proof that your "I am" desire already exists. How else would you have been able to feel it?

In addition to employing the power of e-motion, you can rocket launch your desired intention, setting up an even more magnetic attractor field by using the power of Infinite Love & Gratitude. What feelings could be more appropriate in response to being granted your heart's desires? What more potent emotions could you align yourself with? Feeling Infinite Love & Gratitude to the Universal Source, to yourself, and to life, you enter the realm where the dream takes on a life of its own. Just saying the words has a tremendous positive impact. In fact, you can consider Infinite Love & Gratitude to be the second half of golden rule 2 of manifestation. Once you employ Infinite Love & Gratitude, it's just a matter of time, as you wait for the physical supply train to catch up and deliver.

A Powerful Sign for Darren

During the summer of 1998, my cousin Rob Morgan worked as an intern in my office to prepare to become the first deaf chiropractor to graduate from the Palmer College of

Chiropractic. After watching me work with clients, Rob gave me the "I love you" gesture in American Sign Language. Instantly, a warm, powerful, and peaceful feeling suffused my body. Intrigued by the sensations, I experimented with using muscle testing (a way to discover balance or imbalance within the body via the nervous system) with Rob. Through this technique, I determined that holding the "I love you" hand gesture against weak reflex points on the body actually strengthened them.

Sometime later, I ran across the work of Dr. Masaru Emoto, an alternative-medical researcher in Japan. By studying frozen water crystals under a dark field microscope from water samples that had been exposed to written words like *love, dirty,* and *hate,* he discovered that the vibrational intent of words can positively or negatively affect the structure of water, literally changing their crystalline structure. Of course, since water composes over 70 percent of the human body, he correctly extrapolated that words affect the body as well.

Scientists are discovering that positive emotions like love and appreciation actually regulate heart rate and pull brain waves into more coherent patterns, changes that EKG and EEG machines can read. I incorporated all of this information into the application of The LifeLine Technique that I eventually developed, and over the course of thousands of LifeLine sessions, I've had ample opportunity to witness the astonishing healing effects of both this gesture and the words *Infinite Love & Gratitude,* which are used in both The LifeLine Technique and the shorter See Feel Hear Challenge.

Putting It into Practice

In preparation for doing the See Feel Hear Challenge, let's put the golden rules and the "I love you" American Sign Language gesture into practice. Place your hand in the "I love you" gesture over your heart. Close your eyes, and take time to connect to the present moment. Breathe quietly for a few seconds. Now, listen to your heart and hear what it's telling you. Imagine that you have a menu of infinite possibilities and that right now, your heart can choose to experience and feel anything. Really go for it! And at the same time, simply tune in.

E.G. *I am fulfilled feeling creative*

What's your heart's "Hell yes!"?

Gratitude, love, joy, peace, fulfillment—wherever your heart takes you, it's time to claim it. Say your "I am _____!" intention statement three times out loud, with your hand, again, in the "I love you" gesture over your heart. Embrace the part of you that may be feeling self-conscious or questioning if you're doing it right. Just know that by doing this simple procedure and tapping into your heart space, you're beginning the process of bypassing your limited conscious awareness and gaining access to the buried treasure within your subconscious mind. And if you find it difficult to "feel" anything, that's okay. Everybody filters life differently. If you want to stimulate your feeling sense and ground yourself more deeply in your intention, use your imagination.

Close your eyes and imagine what it's like to be in the land of "I am _____!" Put yourself in the picture in your mind's eye. See the visions that arise. Smell the scents. Hear the words that are spoken as you imagine your intention. What feelings do these inner sights and sounds evoke in your body? Focus on them as if you're already there, and let them slowly expand. Do you suddenly feel peaceful? Excited? Lighter?

Just be with your intention and the feelings it evokes.

This completes the initial steps of the See Feel Hear Challenge. You've deployed the truth question and acknowledged, "Hell no!" you would never consciously choose any illness, pain, fear, and stress. By opening and listening to your heart, focusing on where you're going in a "Hell yes!" way, you've taken the first steps in cracking old, painful patterns. By stirring your imagination to dream, you've awakened your ability to feel—which is an essential step for shifting and awakening a new consciousness. By setting a clear intention to live in alignment with your truth through evoking and using the power of Infinite Love & Gratitude, the stage is set to shift protective subconscious programs by doing the rest of the See Feel Hear Challenge.

Chapter 4

The See Feel Hear Challenge

"By definition, human beings do not see or hear.
Break loose from definition."

— RUMI[1]

Awareness comes in various shapes and sizes. Normal, day-to-day awareness is a highly edited affair, with our beliefs filtering out an enormous percentage of the 11 million bits of information per second that come into our brains, enabling us to function without going nuts from information overload. Our belief systems not only automatically screen out external information, but also simultaneously filter internal information. We disregard the back twinges as we lace up our sneakers, and we ignore the gut-twisting tension accompanying every business meeting. This is all well and good over the short term. But our narrow, day-to-day, pedal-to-the-metal awareness definitely limits us over the long haul.

It's crucial to slow down and tune in to our environment, our relationships, our thought patterns and behavior, as well as our bodies and all their sensations. When we do, we receive vital information that the subconscious has been broadcasting as a means to make us aware all along. How many people spend years racing through life, working and raising a family only to get "sick," discovering in the slow-down period that they hate their jobs, that they want a divorce, and that their souls are urging them to take another path? Taking time to tune in to these extra- and intradimensions of information prompts us to consciously change our lives for the better. And learning how to access these deeper dimensions is exactly what the See Feel Hear Challenge is designed to help us do.

Another Look at Emotion

The See Feel Hear Challenge is a method of digesting and metabolizing emotions, which is kind of an odd statement until you grasp what the words actually mean in this context. As you've already seen, emotion is energy in motion. The word itself even conveys the idea: *e(nergy) motion,* or *e-motion.* The thing that differentiates pure energy from e-motion is thought, which inextricably combines with energy, "coloring" it, imprinting it with the unique flavor of that thought's expression, giving energy the signature frequency of the thought itself.

Thought and emotion come together as a package deal. Think for a moment and see if you can come up with a thought that doesn't have a corresponding feeling. Think about your life, your dog, your job. Think philosophical thoughts. If you take time and really sensitize yourself, you'll discover that each thought has a subtle feeling or emotion attached to it that you can sense throughout your body. Even the thought of having no feeling or emotion has the feeling of emptiness and deadness to it, doesn't it?

Another way to understand how thought and energy are combined is to use the analogy of the invisible very high frequency (VHF) waves that carry audiovisual information to our TV sets. Just as these invisible VHF waves "carry" an embedded signal that our televisions translate into moving pictures, so energy "carries" the thoughts that color it. Every individual thought with its corresponding e-motion (its unique energetic-frequency signature) is translated by the brain, which instantly releases matching chemicals that are then felt in the body as emotions, such as fear, love, hatred, anxiety, and so on. Our thoughts and corresponding emotions not only affect our bodies, but also impact the quantum field, sending out ripples of information that serve as attractor fields drawing matching thoughts, ideas, people, and events to us throughout our lives.

This is great until we react to what we attract! We react with joy, peace, and gratitude to the situations that uplift us, as well as react to the people who cause us to feel frustrated, insecure, and anxious. Either way, the thoughts and attached emotions instantly influence our bodies, for good or for ill. The beat of our hearts changes, our breath quickens or slows, our digestive tracts mobilize, our muscle tone shifts, the pupils of our eyes constrict or dilate, all in response to our thoughts and the e-motions that travel with them.

In 2007 I was experiencing major fatigue, chronic sinus challenges, and asthma. I used a rescue inhaler at least ten times a day. A series of blood tests revealed that I was allergic to gluten, dairy, and eggs—a tough diagnosis for someone who owned a small bakery! Eliminating these foods from my diet was painfully exhausting, and after five years, I decided I no longer needed the "special identity" that food allergies gave me. Dr. Darren guided me through the See Feel Hear Challenge and the emotional digestion of an egg. During the process, I imagined that I was chewing, swallowing, breaking down, and eliminating the egg. At the same time, I was digesting associated emotions, including "unexpressed hurt" and "regret," by seeing, feeling, and hearing them. We harmonized gluten and dairy as well. I left the session and went to my favorite pizza place; ordered a thin-crust, pepperoni and mushroom pizza; and ate every last piece. Since then I've never experienced another physical symptom associated with any food I eat.

— Leslie C.

Repetition of thoughts and their corresponding energy signature (emotions) builds up patterns that either assist or retard health and happiness. Just as the repeating waves of the ocean carve and mold the shoreline, so the repeating waves of thoughts and emotions carve patterns of health or illness into our bodies and relationships. For example, let's say you're putting out a repeating pattern of guilt-based thoughts and emotions. Perhaps these thoughts and emotions affect the muscles and ligaments that hold your shoulder joint in place. You develop a painful rotator-cuff injury that keeps you from being able to do critical physical labor around the house, just when you need to be most helpful to your partner. Where did the injury come from? You think you don't know. You say, "Oh my, what an ill-timed accident! It came out of nowhere!" and go to the doctor to get a prescription for the medication that will relieve you of the pain.

But unless you take the time to go deeper into the injury and ask it to reveal its gift of information, unless you seek greater awareness, the only thing you get out of the situation is discomfort, a doctor's bill, and guess what? More guilt! What a coincidence! Guilt was what started this in the first place. Do you see how the attractor field works? But if you have a tool that will tell you what's really going on, you can interrupt and redirect the cycle, reveal the emotional trigger, and heal at a more profound and permanent level.

Doing the See Feel Hear Challenge

The first step in this process occurs the moment you decide to do it and sit down to take time for yourself, setting aside your phone and other distractions. The next step is about your establishing a connection to the present moment.

Take a few deep, quieting breaths. In this present moment, begin to observe your body and relationships. They form the heart of all authentic dialogue coming from your subconscious mind. Rather than observing your body or relationships as bad, wrong, or broken, simply open a connection to your body and your relationships, and recognize that you are about to engage in an authentic reciprocal conversation. All you have to do is be open to sincere listening.

Begin with your body. Notice the way your body is speaking to you with aches and pains or health concerns. Do you experience tightness in your neck? Sciatic pain? A runny nose? Indigestion? Whatever you observe, write it down on a piece of paper and rate the severity of each of the symptoms on a scale from zero to ten, zero being nothing at all and ten being "Get me off the freakin' planet" (it's that bad).

Example:

- Tight neck muscles: 6
- Sciatic pain in right buttock: 8
- Sinus congestion: 2
- Indigestion: 3

The purpose of rating the symptoms is to create awareness of contrast in your body and to get you dialed in. Write down one primary symptom or multiple symptoms. Whether your body is speaking to you with allergies, constipation, or cancer—whatever is grabbing your attention—be sure to rate the presence of the symptoms on that zero-to-ten scale.

Now switch your attention to your life. You're looking specifically for the relationships and situations in your life that are causing stress or a heavy heart. Notice who or what you immediately think about. Write that person's name or situation down on the paper in front of you—not a whole novel, just a couple of words that acknowledge what or who is causing the stress.

What emotion is associated with this stressor? Think about what happened or is happening in your life that makes this person or circumstance stressful. Feel the immediate reaction you're having to the stressor. Write down the emotion your heart feels as you connect to the person or situation triggering the stress; for example, you lost your job, you got a speeding ticket, your spouse is having an affair, or your child has been diagnosed with autism. After you've written down the emotion, rate it on the zero-to-ten scale. Remember, zero means you feel nothing at all, and ten means you're stressed to the max.

Now that you've observed your body and relationships, take a moment to look at what you wrote down and ask yourself the truth question: "Given the opportunity for me to create my life, a day, or a moment in time, would I ever choose to feel this way in my body or in my life?" Answer the question out loud from your heart as if you mean it: "Hell no!"

Knowing that you would never choose any pain, fear, or stress is incredibly empowering. It's also an acknowledgment of the subconscious mind's role in your life. Remember, the subconscious mind never chooses and never judges. It only reacts to protect a part of you that didn't have the tools, strategies, and support that you currently have.

Now it's time to set an intention. Follow the two golden rules of manifesting an intention, and go into your heart and listen to what it truly desires to feel right now. Acknowledge the menu of infinite possibilities, and allow your heart to choose an intention in a "Hell yes!" way. Write down this intention. The simpler you can make this intention, the better (for example, pure love, gratitude, juicy joy, and so on). Write whatever your heart chooses. Now put the words *I am* in front of that on your piece of paper to acknowledge oneness with your intent, and say your intention as an

49

"I am" statement three times out loud with your hand in the "I love you" gesture over your heart: for example, "I am pure love, I am pure love, I am pure love."

This is your intention. This vibration will be used to guide, reflect, and empower a subconsciously protective part of you to grow, change, and evolve. For this to happen, you must first be open and willing to use your imagination, so acknowledge to yourself that you are prepared to do so.

Take your time and use your imagination to witness yourself in the land of "I am pure love" (or whatever your intention is). Write down the feeling you get as you imagine this. If you're really into imagining it, you'll notice that it feels empowering, awesome, great, fabulous. If you're not really into imagining and feeling it, you'll write down words like *okay, good,* or *nice.* If you came up with words like this, you need to go back to the drawing board! Remember, everything that exists is born from imagination!

Let's say the feeling that comes up is *awesome.*

You now have a completed intention statement: "I am *pure love* feeling *awesome!*"

The See Feel Hear Section of the Challenge

Now it's time to do the See Feel Hear (SFH) Challenge. There's a three-prong approach to every SFH process: (1) processing physical symptoms, (2) processing stressful circumstances, and (3) processing the intention. Each aspect—the physical symptoms, the emotional stressor, and the intention—is processed via seeing, feeling, and hearing what your subconscious has to say.

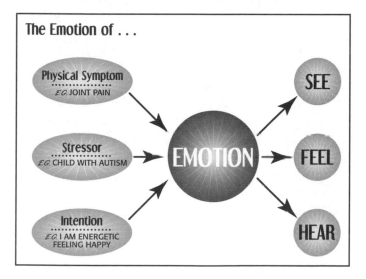

1. First you process the physical symptoms. Connect to the list of physical symptoms that your body is speaking with. What emotion comes up as you observe and acknowledge the symptoms that your body is expressing? Whatever the emotion—anger, fear, sadness, and so on—as soon as you can label it, put your hand in the "I love you" gesture over your heart and say, "Infinite Love & Gratitude" to this emotion; for example, "Infinite Love & Gratitude to fear."

A. Now *See* the thoughts, memories, and images that immediately begin to show up in your mind's eye in relation to fear. As they show up, fill your heart with Infinite Love & Gratitude. Put your hand in the "I love you" gesture over your heart. Say, "Infinite Love & Gratitude to the images in your mind associated with fear. Infinite Love & Gratitude." Say it several times until you perceive a shift in the fearful thoughts you're seeing.

B. Allow yourself to *Feel* what it's like in your body to experience fear. Acknowledge the quality and intensity of this fear feeling. As you are noticing what fear feels like, put your hand in the "I love you" gesture over your heart and say "Infinite Love & Gratitude to feeling fear. Infinite Love & Gratitude." Say it several times as you focus on the feeling, until you notice a shift. Trust the process; it will happen.

C. *Hear* the voice of fear that stems from observing the symptoms in your body. What belief does fear hold about your body? What does it have to say? For example, "I don't deserve love," or "Have faith in yourself." As you listen, put your hand in the "I love you" gesture over your heart and say, "Infinite Love & Gratitude to the voice of fear. Infinite Love & Gratitude," until you notice a shift.

2. Now you're ready to process the emotion that you feel is associated with situations causing you stress. What emotion comes up as you observe and acknowledge the stressful people or circumstances in your life? Let's say you're feeling frustrated with a co-worker. Ask yourself, "What emotion do I feel as a result of that frustration?" Let's say anger comes up.

Now we want to process the anger through the See Feel Hear Challenge.

A. *See* the angry thoughts associated with the stressful relationship. Observe the images and memories that spontaneously come up that are associated with the anger. Put your hand in the "I love you" gesture over your heart and say "Infinite Love & Gratitude to seeing anger. Infinite Love & Gratitude," until you sense a shift in what you're seeing.

B. Allow yourself to *Feel* the anger that's associated with being frustrated. Put your hand in the "I love you" gesture over your heart. Repeat, "Infinite Love & Gratitude to feeling anger. Infinite Love & Gratitude," until you sense a shift in the feeling of anger.

C. *Hear* the voice of anger stemming from the frustration. Hear the beliefs of anger. As you're hearing that voice, put your hand in the "I love you" gesture over your heart and say, "Infinite Love & Gratitude to the voice of anger. Infinite Love & Gratitude," until you sense a shift.

3. Now we want to process the intention. Connect with your intention statement, "I am pure love, feeling awesome." Observe the emotion that you feel as a result of tuning in to your intention. It could be joyful, confident, doubtful, ashamed, and so on. Let's say it's joyful. Say, "Infinite Love & Gratitude to joyful. Infinite Love & Gratitude."

A. *See* the joyful thoughts associated with your intention. Observe the images that spontaneously come up. Put your hand in the "I love you" gesture over your heart and say, "Infinite Love & Gratitude to seeing joyful. Infinite Love & Gratitude," until you observe a shift.

B. Allow yourself to *Feel* joyful associated with setting an intention of "I am pure love feeling awesome." Put your hand in the "I love you" gesture over your heart. Say, "Infinite Love & Gratitude to feeling joyful. Infinite Love & Gratitude," until you sense a shift.

C. *Hear* the voice of joyful stemming from living with intention. Hear the beliefs of joyful. As you're hearing that voice, put your hand in the "I love you" gesture over your heart. Say, "Infinite Love & Gratitude to the voice of joy. Infinite Love & Gratitude," until you feel a shift.

Take a moment to observe how it feels to be present in the moment. Notice how your body feels. Does it feel the same as when you began? Go back and connect to the circumstance or the relationship that was causing you to feel stress. How does it feel to connect with that person or circumstance now? Take the time to really enjoy the present moment and the "new you."

Darren's 28-Day Challenge

The See Feel Hear Challenge is truly a practice. The more you commit yourself to using it, the more you train your brain, body, and behavior with conscious intention, the better off you and your life are. So take me up on my challenge, and commit yourself to doing the SFH once per day for 28 days.

It will change your life!

Although you don't have to, I encourage you to do the three-prong approach each time, addressing each physical symptom, stressor, and intention. The patterns that are happening in your personal

relationships and the relationships happening between the cells of your body are all interconnected. And why miss an opportunity to process an intention? The more you practice all three
prongs of this process, the more comfortable and
confident you will be at identifying these emotional
patterns in yourself and others.

A Postscript about Emotions

A lot of people have a hard time connecting to their
emotions. It's no one's fault. It's just the conditioning of
the society we're all part of. But being able to consciously
connect to the subtleties of emotion is the cornerstone
to creating significant shifts in our lives. Emotion am-
plifies creative intention. By focusing on where we're
going rather than what we want to get rid of, we shift
subconscious protective patterns into conscious acts of
growth. We move into present-time consciousness. By
being willing to consciously feel and move through pain
and suffering, we come to the beautiful place where we
experience love, oneness, life force, and authentic flow.
Caring enough to seek genuine understanding and healing, we begin to experience the following characteristics:

Compassionate communication
Authenticity
Rapport
Empowerment

Not only is the See Feel Hear Challenge wonderful for health and healing, but it's also a highly effective tool for consciously improving work, social, and personal relationships. And it's not just about solving so-called problems. We'll also show how you can apply it as a wonderful manifestation tool. In the next part of the book, we'll look at some very interesting scientific reasons why and how the See Feel Hear Challenge is so effective.

Part II

HOW AND WHY
IT WORKS

Chapter 5

The Power of the Heart

"Whoever finds love beneath hurt and grief
disappears into emptiness with a thousand new disguises."

— RUMI[1]

We are the sum total of our experience, and the heart of the matter is that our bodies hold the key. Every experience we've had from conception onward, everything we've ever thought and felt, is still with us, imprinted in the neurons of our brains—a vast subconscious storehouse of information and memories.

Whatever the actual mechanism, it's impossible to deny that the body is the communication channel between the subconscious and conscious minds. The body gives us signals, telling us what to pay attention to through a wide variety of feelings, sensations, and symptoms. It provides the retrieval system for the images, feelings, and thoughts that the See Feel Hear Challenge evokes. And finally, it is the place where healing naturally occurs.

What Is Healing?

But what really is healing? What does it entail? What is the state of health, and how do we access it? As much as we like the idea of the magic bullet, the pill, the doctor, and the prescription that will instantly cure our ills, there's nothing outside of us that does the healing. "Natural forces within us are the true healers of disease," wrote Hippocrates, the father of modern medicine, back in the 5th century B.C.E. The World Health Organization (WHO) defines health as, "a complete state of physical, mental, and social well-being, and not merely the absence of disease or infirmity."[2] So if health as a state of well-being and healing is a process of aligning with the natural forces within us, doesn't it make sense that attaining and maintaining health and well-being is simply a process of understanding what's natural for us and aligning with it?

Absolutely! Unfortunately, there's little in the modern lifestyle that's very natural anymore. Our days start with us on the run, sucking down lattes and sugar-laden breakfast foods. Then we sit in stop-and-go traffic before being crammed into hermetically sealed offices, where toxins from synthetic construction materials, furniture, and cleaning products circulate through ventilation systems in buildings, manifesting something environmental engineers call "sick building syndrome."

A co-worker one-ups us in front of the boss. We get put on a tight production deadline. Already stressed, we go into emotional high gear. The "fight-or-flight" response—originally designed to briefly kick in to get us away from the saber-toothed tiger and safely back to our caves, where we companionably hunkered down at the end of a long day of healthy physical exercise around a crackling fire with our families and tribes to eat simple roots, berries, and whatever meat or fish we could kill or catch—is now stuck permanently in the "on" position.

The return commute does nothing to ease the stress, nor does the pile of bills waiting on the kitchen table, where our equally stressed partner sets out another meal of genetically modified, chemically treated agribusiness food from the grocery store. The labels say, "All Natural." But hey, cyanide is natural! Or maybe we go to a bar to unwind or go to speed dating. At bedtime we relax with a violent TV show and shocking footage on the news. Then we get up the next morning and repeat the same stress cycle all over again.

Is it any wonder that we've lost our health and well-being and can no longer easily grasp what's "natural" and good for us? Fortunately for us, there's a health indicator built right into our bodies. The greatest diagnostic and healing tool ever designed lies right in our chests!

The Power of the Heart

Beating in tune with the resonant frequency of the Earth herself, the heart is far more than a muscle that pumps blood through our circulatory systems. In many ancient cultures, it was viewed as the source of a warrior's strength. Heart extraction was a frequent form of sacrifice in the Aztec culture of Mesoamerica, for this organ was considered to be the seat of a person's soul, containing the heat of the sun itself. This process allowed the person, liberated by the sacrifice, a guaranteed seat in heaven. In ancient Egyptian death rites, the heart was measured against the weight of a feather on the scales of Ma'at during divine judgment. If the person's heart was unburdened by negative emotions and light enough to balance the feather, then she or he would move on into the eternal afterlife.

Talk about heavy furniture!

The human heart has long been recognized as the seat of feelings, especially love. And the belief that our hearts often know the truth better than our brains is still a popular one. The Greek philosopher Plato taught that feeling and thinking were completely separate functions of the soul that were usually in conflict with one another. In his view, feelings and emotions were unruly and in dire need of being harnessed by the intellect—a philosophy still visible in society's preference for scientific rationalism and intellectualism today.

Neuroscience is proving Plato right about our emotions and intellectual functioning being two separate systems. However, the latest discoveries are bumping the brain off its pedestal as the supreme ruler of physiological functions, perception, thought, and emotion. Neuroscientists now know that the brain and the heart are intricately interconnected, and that the heart has its own "intelligence" that is not dictated by the brain. In fact, it's often the other way around. Neurocardiologists have discovered that the heart has its own internal nervous system, and scientists at the Institute of HeartMath, a nonprofit research and education organization based in California, go so far as to say that this plexus of nerves containing over 40,000 neurons is the "'little brain' [that] gives the heart the ability to independently sense, process information, make decisions, and even demonstrate a type of learning and memory."

Score one for the hopeless romantics who believe the heart knows best!

The heart generates the largest electromagnetic field in the body, approximately 60 times greater than the electrical amplitude of the brain's field.[3] There are more and denser neural communication pathways connecting the heart to the brain than vice versa. Furthermore, the heart's messages to the brain have been found to directly change perceptions and affect how we think, what we feel, and how we perform. The heart's neurological signals directly affect the amygdala, the center of emotional processing in the brain, and can trigger responses in the autonomic nervous system before the rest of the brain can process the incoming sensory information.

In other words, our hearts can hijack us and take us for a ride!

Since 1991, the Institute of HeartMath (IHM) has been conducting research in stress management and the innate intelligence of the heart. This research consistently affirms the power of the heart to generate emotional experiences and its ability to interact with and regulate other systems in the body:

> With every beat, the heart not only pumps blood, but also transmits complex patterns of neurological, hormonal, pressure, and electromagnetic information to the brain and throughout the body. As a critical nodal point in many of the body's interacting systems, the heart is uniquely positioned as a powerful entry point into the communication network that connects body, mind, emotions, and spirit.

The heart is the most powerful regulating organ in the body, and the field generated by the human heart is so strong that a magnetometer can detect it from over ten feet away. Not only does the heart influence the brain, but a person's heart field can actually affect another person's brain-wave patterns if the two people physically touch or are even in close proximity.[4]

The Heart's Role in Healing

By studying heart rate variability (HRV) patterns in electrocardiograms, scientists have been able to literally read the differences between healthy, positive emotions and detrimental, negative ones. In negative states, the HRV patterns are chaotic and jerky. When emotions like love, appreciation, and caring are being expressed, the resulting HRV patterns are coherent and ordered.

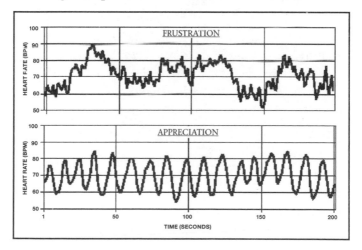

Studies also show that when our minds and emotions are out of sync, overall system coherence and perceptual awareness decrease. When they are in sync, overall coherence and awareness increase. In other words, when our hearts and our minds are aligned, we enter a state of inner harmony and keenness known as "the zone": we become conscious. Vision and hearing improve, the mind is clear, and reaction time is razor sharp. We feel fluid, strong, and at peace. In the zone, it's the powerful heart, not the mind, that's leading the show.

> My daughter came home from school today feeling super angry. She was able to connect to the emotion through the SFH Challenge and process the experience. Her mood totally shifted, and moments later she burst into song about infinite love and gratitude! I am so unspeakably grateful for the See Feel Hear Challenge. It's incredibly grounding and simultaneously uplifting for me—such a tremendous gift!
>
> — Erica H.

This is why, when it comes to initiating physical or mental healing, implementing change, creating a healthy lifestyle, or manifesting something we want, the power of positive thinking just isn't enough to get the job done. Emotions are a far more powerful influence on the brain than thought when it comes to shifting our mental processes and patterns. Great strides in stress management are being accomplished through training people to induce positive, coherent emotions within themselves—which is part of the See Feel Hear Challenge. Once the positive emotions are felt, the mind is automatically brought into alignment. As Doc Childre, founder of the Institute of HeartMath, puts it, "It takes a power stronger than the mind to bend perception, override emotional circuitry, and provide us with intuitive feeling instead. It takes the power of the heart."

When you set your intention during the See Feel Hear Challenge and imagine already being what it is that you desire, whether it's feeling buoyantly loving in a new relationship or having your body feel lithe and flexible during yoga sessions, once your mind and heart are in sync with the conscious power of the new intention, some amazing things happen. Your heart's electromagnetic field immediately begins to resonate at the frequency of the *feeling* of what you're experiencing in your imagination. By imagining and feeling love, for example, you literally pump the frequency of love into the quantum sea, setting up an attractor field that will pull to you just the person who will evoke the exact frequency you're emanating. Not only that, while sitting there bathed in that wonderful emotion, you're positively affecting the world around you.

Rating Consciousness

Through extensive research using applied kinesiology (a diagnostic tool that uses muscle testing as an information-feedback mechanism), the late physician, researcher, and psychiatrist Dr. David R. Hawkins determined that different levels of consciousness emanate different levels of energetic-attractor fields.[5] Testing and calibrating a wide range of consciousness states on a scale ranging from 1 to 1,000, the lowest-frequency state he discovered was shame, which registers at a level of 20. In contrast, the highest state of consciousness available to humans, enlightenment, registers at frequencies between 700 and 1,000.

The greater the state of consciousness, the more powerful the attractor field that's created, and the greater the number of people in the world who are affected. For example, if you're sitting in your living room emanating love, which calibrates at 500, you're producing a field strong enough to counterbalance approximately 750,000 people operating at a consciousness level below 200, the calibrated strength of courage that Hawkins estimates is the "break-even point" of consciousness between lower negative frequencies and higher levels of consciousness.

So what happens when you do the See Feel Hear Challenge?

Say you're living in a state of frustration over past love affairs gone wrong. You're filled with disappointment and desires (cravings) for love, and you feel empty inside. On Hawkins's consciousness scale, you're operating at a level of 125, literally being a drag on yourself and the rest of humanity. But as soon as you ask the truth question, "Would I ever choose to feel this way?" arrive at the logical answer, "Hell no!" and set your intention to love, everything changes. Your imagination kicks into gear. Mind and heart synchronize. You start feeling the emotion of love, and presto! Your whole world changes, and so does the consciousness of a lot of other people you don't even know. Talk about a win-win situation! And other magical things happen when the heart gets to do its thing as well.

Maybe you suffer from arthritis yet dream about running the Chicago Marathon. Doing the See Feel Hear Challenge, rather than focusing on the arthritic pain, you set your intention and fire up your imagination, seeing and feeling yourself running the marathon. You can even hear the rush of feet all around you on the pavement! As you sit there, imagining the race, you sense limber muscles gliding effortlessly beneath the fascia as you run. You feel the excitement and ease in your body. And guess what? As you're doing this, your heart starts producing something called *imaginal cells* that literally start building the physical foundation in your body for your dream to come true!

Similar to *stem cells* (undifferentiated cells found in the human body that can be extracted and planted into injured areas to become healthy heart cells, skin cells, liver cells, or whatever is needed in the affected area), imaginal cells are also "unprogrammed" cells that can transform themselves to take over a wide variety of physiological functions. Originally discovered in insects such as beetles, butterflies, and two-winged flies, imaginal cells are found during the metamorphosis between the pupal stage of the insect and the final adult stage, called the *imago,* that which has been imagined to be: the ugly worm transformed into the moth or the butterfly.[6]

It's no coincidence that imaginal cells can also be found in the human heart. The heart even looks a little like a chrysalis: a chalice waiting to consciously contain our deepest dreams that is also magnificently designed to create both imaginal cells and the electromagnetic fields that can make those dreams come true. Whether butterfly or beetle, marathon runner or lover, the power of intentional imagination is what transforms lives. And the heart is the essential ingredient of the becoming process.

What's Your Heart's Desire?

Just for a little while, forget practicality. Ignore what your mind and your mother have to say. Take time out to get in touch with your heart's deepest desires—not just the cool things you've always wanted to do, like surf the left-hand point-break curl in Peru, but your innermost heart's secret desires.

Of course, maybe deep in your heart you've always wanted to be that surfer dude—the free vagabond exploring the world. Or maybe you've dreamed of being a filmmaker, or maybe a teacher in Africa. Maybe you want to adopt a refugee child or get a divorce or start your own business.

Listen to your heart. It might not be calling you to the easiest path in the world. There may be emotional blocks apparently standing in the way that need processing with the See feel Hear Challenge. There may be difficulties and hardships. But listen to what's really calling you. If you pay attention, your heart will always point toward the highest, best, most evolutionary path for you.

Chapter 6

The Mind as a
Tool for Change

"An eye is meant to see things.
The soul is here for its own joy.
A head has one use: for loving a true love.
Legs: to run after."

— RUMI[1]

The mind is the aspect of our being that results from perceptions gleaned through our sense organs and co-ordinated by the brain into thoughts. Because the mind is invisible, intangible, and abstract, we tend to isolate "mind" as something apart from the body. But would we have thoughts if we had no senses? No eyes to take cues from the environment? No ears to hear language? No physical sensations to communicate through?

"Once I knew only darkness and stillness. My life was without past or future," said Helen Keller. "But a little word from the fingers of another fell into my hand that clutched at emptiness, and my heart leaped to the rapture of living." Given sufficient physical information, Keller vaulted from isolated deaf-mute onto the world stage as a noted speaker, author, social reformer, and suffragette, praised as one of the foremost minds of the early 20th century. Without sufficient physical input, however, her mind would have remained shrouded in darkness.

The mind and body are not separate from one another. Rather, they are congruent aspects of existence, constantly informing one another. As wind creates ripples in the sand, the patterns of the mind directly influence the cycles and rhythms of the body. The body speaks the mind, with the physical functions and form of the body reflecting the particular lens of consciousness that the mind is projecting: ease versus "dis-ease," action versus reaction, love versus fear. But ultimately we are neither the mind nor the body.

The mind is a tool, or at least it has the potential to be. Unfortunately, because mind and body are so inextricably linked and overwhelmingly the center of our experience, we end up identifying with both. But mistaking "self" for either one is rather like mistaking a hammer for the carpenter who wields it. Mind-body is a manifestation in time-space and the means through which creation is made known in an astounding and wonderful journey. But when we lose ourselves on the trip (and all of us do!) by thinking that we are the mind-body, we end up falling down all sorts of rabbit holes.

It's easy to get lost, because all that we know from birth onward is the body experience. Initially, our world is comprised of flashes of color, faces, voices, the softness of a blanket, the sticky wetness and flavor of milk, the discomfort of an unchanged diaper. Inescapably, we identify with the body. It's all we know! Swiftly the mind component grows, and we develop language, communication, social interactions, and mental self-talk. By the time we enter first grade, we're unconsciously convinced that "Mind-Body R Us."

We answer questions such as, "Who are you?" in predictably physical terms. "I'm a human being," we say. Or "I'm a girl or a boy. I'm African-American or Hispanic or Caucasian." We respond that we're a certain age, build, or appearance. If we're daring, we admit our sexual preference. We mention our careers and our social roles, our religions and our philosophies, our attitudes and our so-called problems as if all of these things were what we are. *But they're just what we think we are.* Marine biologist, unemployed, feminist, atheist, alcoholic, Catholic—we fill our résumés and Facebook pages with these ideas about ourselves so that people can get a handle on who we believe ourselves to be.

The Neurological Network of Identity

Despite massive core beliefs to the contrary, the individual human identity that we call George, Jane, or Harold is really just a limited thought form organized from sense-based information that impinges upon the brain over time. It's a mind-set: an inevitable way of thinking that comes from being birthed into a physical body, a mirage grounded in social beliefs that tell us that's all we are, a firing pattern of neurons in the brain mixed with vague soul urgings and spiritual impulses. And each new sensual experience provides evidence that we are what we believe ourselves to be. Why? Because everything gets filtered through the neurological network of what's already known and accepted. And this entire self-proving subconscious process gives us "reality" and "identity."

What a ride!

The See Feel Hear Challenge helps me to express and transform emotional reactions into opportunities to become more present and play an active role in my life. I am able to write my own

> "script" instead of always reacting like a puppet on a string. The process is a blessing in my life each and every day.
>
> — Tim N.

Tossing the truth question into this mix is rather like detonating an explosive device. It vaults us out of our hypnotic identification with the mind-body, giving us access to the impartial observer. From this more-detached mental space, we regather the reins of choice. And once we start engaging choice, we start asking ourselves interesting questions like, "Who's making this choice?" and "Why do I choose the way I do?" We start observing reactive behavior patterns and begin hearing the voices of our programmed identity. We discover where we want to create shifts. When we get in touch with our heart, our authentic self shows up. Through setting an intention from this space and doing the See Feel Hear Challenge, we begin using the mind-body as the tool it was designed to be: an incredibly conscious manifester that helps us experience what our hearts know to be our deeper truth.

Getting Right with the Mind

For us to have richly fulfilling lives, neither heart nor mind alone is enough. We need both clarity of mind and a certain conscious discernment of feeling to make life work well.

The Noble Eightfold Path to the end of human suffering created by Siddhartha Gautama, the Buddha, in the 6th century B.C.E. leans heavily on getting "right" with the mind. The first principle, developing Right View, basically means accepting that suffering in life is inevitable until you release attachment to transient things, including your personal identity. The second principle, Right Intention, is about making a promise to yourself to live differently, to make volitional choices that lead to happiness instead of suffering. All the other principles—Right Mindfulness, Right Concentration, Right Effort, Right Livelihood, Right Action, and Right Speech—follow from the first two principles.

The See Feel Hear Challenge is a challenge, not because it's difficult to do, but because it challenges our perception of suffering. Don't you know we're attached to that! We get mileage out of suffering and take it on as an identity. We merge with insecurity, unhappiness, and depression to such a degree that we think that's what we are. But the truth question wakes us up to the fact that suffering is not inevitable. The very act of asking the truth question sets the ball in motion to obtain Right View and Right Intention.

Right Mindfulness and all the other principles automatically fall into place as we begin to consciously choose happiness, health, a house, a job, a mate, and the overall design of who we want to be. Following our heart's desires, we begin to use our minds as an appropriate tool—imagining what we want in the greatest possible detail, intentionally evoking feelings to maximally impact the quantum field to draw our heart's desires to us. Imagining and feeling, we clearly grasp as a lived experience where our imagined experiences and goals will take us. In other words, choice gets easier.

Let's say you're having difficulty choosing a house to rent. Should it be the more economical condo? Or the larger, more expensive house with the view? You can afford either one. Your heart tugs at you and steers you toward the larger house. But you've got doubts and fears about money that direct you toward the cheaper condo. Instead of letting fear automatically run the show and make the decision for you, you process the fear through the See Feel Hear Challenge. You put the mind-body to work and imagine living in the condo. You note the sensations, how it feels. *Hmm, it feels a little cramped and claustrophobic.* You imagine living in the larger house with the view and experience feelings of expansiveness and harmony. Armed with this subtle but vital information that reflects your future relationship with both dwellings, you are free to make a conscious choice about where you want to be. This is putting the mind-body to conscious use and action!

Thinking vs. Being

Having intellectual knowledge about something doesn't bestow wisdom any more than knowing that the brain is capable of creating and releasing endorphins to mitigate pain gets rid of a headache. It's an interesting fact with great potential. But when it comes to a headache, most people still tend to reach for the aspirin bottle. Similarly, we can think things like *I am abundant* all day long and never become wealthy, because we haven't learned how to *be* the condition of wealth any more than we have learned how to *be* so in tune with our brain processes that we can stimulate endorphin production at will.

If you have angst over the price of chicken in the grocery store or feel a flicker of fear as you open your online bank statement, wealth simply can't happen. Your state of *being* is preoccupied with subconscious fears about money, about not having enough. If you don't realize this, you can never change the program. This is why it's so important to pay attention to emotional cues when they show up.

If your heart yearns for the spaciousness of a larger home and yet fear drives you to take the small condo, this is a wonderful opportunity to address unprocessed emotional patterns of financial insecurity. And when you do, you not only free yourself of an old, limiting program, but you also shift your financial destiny to one of greater potential. You rent the more-spacious house that matches your new, spacious way of being, and all goes well.

Now let's look at the other possible path. Remember, subconscious programs emanate a frequency that draws matching circumstances and emotions to you so that they can be recognized. So what are the ramifications of not processing the subconscious financial fears and not putting the mind-body to work? You reactively settle for the condo. Because it's not what your heart truly desires, you end up feeling depressed living there. Your body begins to speak to you with symptoms. You get sick. You lose your job. You lose the condo. Everything you feared would happen if you had rented the larger house occurs.

Being is not a mental process—far from it! Our minds are merely tools framing our desires. Once our intentions are formed, a passionate shift into the heart and feeling must occur. You can *think* about getting your pilot's license, but that doesn't make you a pilot. To do that, you must embody the knowledge, the sensations, the attitude, and the feelings of flying a plane. To *be* something, you've got to take all of yourself along on the ride.

Intuition and Seeing, Feeling, and Hearing

Quantum physics has proven that we dwell in a sea of undifferentiated energy uniting the universe. Noted English mathematical physicist Sir Roger Penrose has taken things even farther. He theorizes that at the level of the *Planck scale* (an unfathomably small and unimaginably energetic scale at which even quantum field theory breaks down), the entire universe is actually pure abstract information. This level of information is not information in the sense that we normally consider it. It's not words or binary code or electromagnetic waves carrying pictures and music. Even microwaves are positively gigantic compared to the Planck scale. As Penrose envisions it, the Planck scale is the abstract realm of ideals that Plato talked about: an absolute intangible "world" of absolute truths and aesthetic beauty, coherence, and mathematical geometry from which the physical world is derived and formed.[2]

If creation is indeed information based, and information permeates everything, as a part of creation you would imagine that human beings would be able to receive all of this information. And we can! If we learn to not just look but to see, to listen and really hear, to sense and feel the lay of the land in any given situation, whole new worlds of information open up to us. And the See Feel Hear Challenge helps us do just that.

When we vault beyond the frequently considerable strife of circumstances and use the See Feel Hear Challenge to elevate our consciousness through the visual, kinesthetic, and auditory centers of our brains, when we set a new intention, when we move past the suffering, our conscious and subconscious mind fields harmonize. Our chakras and the primary and secondary acupuncture meridians coordinate, and our intuition naturally increases. In this refined space, we open ourselves to receiving information from the quantum sea or the Planck scale. We sense things we aren't generally privy to, developing *ESP* (extrasensory perception that enables us to communicate with the subtle energy world outside) and *ISP* (intrasensory perception that enables us to communicate with the subtle energy world within us).

Attuned to the inner voice via the quantum field, we're also able to receive information from others. We're talking, and we hear a companion's unspoken words. We see beyond the person's flesh to the inner person. As we empathically feel the other person's emotions, compassion blossoms within us. We begin to see, feel, and hear situations differently. The child failing in school, the unsatisfying marriage, the diseased person, the struggling business—all take on new dimensions of meaning and possibility. Responding with expanded information instead of reacting, we begin to think more wisely, speak more kindly, and act more sustainably.

"We were born to make manifest the glory of God that exists within us," writes Marianne Williamson. "It's not just in some of us; it's in everyone!" Ultimately, this beautiful, awakened state is the change that we all seek: to go beyond our current limitations to embrace a broader vision and definition of our humanity, seeking not only a new and better life for ourselves, but also a new, better life for others. As we desire change, embrace awareness, and do the work we must do to elevate ourselves, our minds become full and a new reality dawns, blessing us with its grace and abundance.

Fantasy: The Fastest Road to Being

In case you have any doubts about the power of the mind to affect reality, consider this: what happens when you have a sexual fantasy?

Your body turns on. Right? Well, it's the same way with the rest of life.

The best possible road to learning how to "be," whether it's turned on, wealthy, healthy, or wise, is to fantasize about it—really! So choose something you want to experience: a mate, a new home, a world cruise, whatever. Make a detailed list describing the setting, situation, or person. Keep a running internal check as you make your list. What makes you feel tantalized? What makes you feel warm and fuzzy? Excited?

When you go to bed at night, instead of lying awake worrying about whether you armed the alarm system, take yourself to fantasyland. Imagine doing, having, seeing, smelling, hearing, touching, and tasting what you desire. Build your dream! Play with it! (Remember, as a kid you did this all the time.) Let yourself get excited. The more feeling that's evoked in your body, the more effective the fantasy will be and the stronger the impact.

Feel what it's like to have and do what you desire. This is "being it."

Now you have a better understanding of the science of the heart, mind, and emotions and the effectiveness of "being" what it is you desire—all the underlying mechanics of the See Feel Hear Challenge. In the next part of the book, we'll examine some of the things that might stand in the way of your caring enough about yourself to use the Challenge to change your life.

Part III

CHALLENGES
TO CHOOSING A
PURPOSEFUL LIFE

Chapter 7

What's Wrong with Now?

"This is now. Now is all there is. Don't wait for Then;
strike the spark, light the fire. Sit at the Beloved's table,
feast with gusto, drink your fill then dance the way branches
of jasmine and cypress dance in a spring wind."

— R U M I [1]

Present-time consciousness (PTC) contains everything we truly desire: connection, love, belonging, authenticity, acceptance, grace, happiness, and peace. All the things we want to feel and experience are just waiting for us to show up. But only if we're in PTC are we capable of choosing and then deeply experiencing those e-motions.

The now is an intense state of wakefulness to our internal and external conditions. We don't just feel the sun on our faces and inhale the scents of mowed grass and charcoal barbeques. We're *aware of being aware* that we're feeling the sun and inhaling the summer scents. We're in tune with our body's rhythms, and we know what emotions we're experiencing. We're present to it all.

The difference between normal waking consciousness and PTC is kind of like the difference between lying in bed dreaming and standing in front of the mirror the next morning as you brush your teeth. While dreaming, you have little or no choice. Even if the dream is taking you over a cliff while you scream in terror, you're in the "dreamscape," and there's no stopping what's happening.

Once you wake up, of course, the involuntary ride is over. The dream is gone. You have choice. You get up, chuckling over the silliness of being so scared; set the dream aside; and get on with doing the things you have to do. You aren't aware that you shift your attention and your emotions. It isn't conscious. You don't choose it. You just do it. So is the dream really over? Not really! As the 19th-century American poet Edgar Allan Poe put it, "All that we see or seem is but a dream within a dream."

In both normal waking consciousness and in dreams, we rarely have any control unless we do something to consciously initiate it. We're simply along for the ride, reacting to life as subconscious programs are triggered. But as soon as we become aware of our condition, that changes. In the morning, when our dreams fade, we "wake up" and enter a state of relative lucidity. We're aware that we've been dreaming, and we realize we've entered a whole new realm of consciousness. Unfortunately, we fail to realize that, at another level, we're still asleep!

If we awaken in the dream state itself, we enter a state of consciousness called "lucid dreaming." If we awaken while we're "awake" and become lucid, we enter present-time consciousness. In both states, we now have choice and can affect the conditions of the environment in which we discover ourselves. In the lucid dream, we can choose where we want the dream to go, change the environment, fly, and do whatever we can imagine. Caught up in the novelty and excitement of the experience, we rarely choose how we're feeling throughout the lucid-dream experience. In the waking state of PTC, we may not be able to instantly change our external environment and fly, but we can definitely take control and make conscious choices about how we feel in the moment and where our lives are headed.

The shift into lucidity in both cases is simple, instantaneous, and satisfying. So why don't we access PTC more often? Why does the now seem so elusive?

The Winter of Discontent

Have you ever noticed how difficult it is to be happy with what you've got? How happiness always seems to be just around the corner, awaiting graduation day, a smaller dress size, or the new car? Whether we're anxiously longing for "the One" to come along and sweep us off our feet or the job promotion that'll give us more money, we're almost always longing for something other than what we've got. We want to live everywhere but in the present moment, as we are, where we are. Even though it actually contains everything we could ever want, we act as if the now contained nothing!

> The See Feel Hear Challenge is such a simple and effective way to embrace emotions, and it always brings me immediate physical relief, clarity, and insight!
>
> — Alison C.

The list of things we aren't and haven't got is endless. We live in a state of chronic discontent that, for most of us, is a core condition that started when we were very young. As a kid, didn't you wish to be bigger; smarter; better in gym; and a fourth grader, an eighth grader, or

a senior? Didn't you want a better bike, a faster computer, nicer parents, and no zits so that the really cute girls
or boys would date you? Didn't you want later curfews?
How about a driver's license with a date on it that meant
you wouldn't get kicked out of the bar if you were carded?

Have things changed all that much since then, ex-
cept maybe the price tags on what you want? Or perhaps
now you wish the date on your driver's license would
reverse gears?

The media massages our dissatisfactions, feeding
the frenzy inside us to be somehow different and better.
TV and magazines promote glitzy lifestyles of the rich
and famous. Reality shows zero in on our insecurities,
highlighting extreme makeovers from hair to clothing
to career to lifestyle changes. Millions watch as fantasies
are fulfilled, talent is discovered, spouses are swapped,
and fat people lumber through humiliating weight-loss
exercises to become the world's *Biggest Loser*—all just to
satisfy the deep craving to be somehow special and different from what we already are.

Photoshop Reality

Everyone is already special just as they are. But we
live in a Photoshop reality, where even the world's top
supermodels, like Lara Stone, are regularly subjected to
electronic beauty enhancement. Blemishes and freckles

are removed; eyes are made larger and brighter, lips redder and fuller; busts are increased, necks elongated, cheek-bones enhanced; waistlines and thighs are reduced; cellulite is eradicated; and derrieres are sculpted into fine art pieces. Actors and sports stars look gorgeously fit and wholesome even if they've just crawled out of detox.

We're constantly barraged with images of airbrushed perfection. Every advertisement in every magazine has been retouched, and sometimes the models used in these ads bear little resemblance to themselves in the final version. For example, in a series of ads for Bulgari handbags, actress Julianne Moore, an attractive, freckled redhead, is turned into an alabaster Leda-and-the-Swan–type beauty, naked but for a strategically placed white cockatoo and a handbag. Dark-red hair, perfect white skin, sculpted shoulders so thin she seems anorexic, Moore is virtually unrecognizable.

We wanted to use several before-and-after photos in this book as examples. But, as you can see, the final Photoshop example we've included is definitely not of Julianne Moore! Neither Bulgari nor any other advertiser we approached would give us reprint permission to use their ads in this book. Nor could we get permission from various magazine publications to reprint cover photos that had been extensively retouched.

It's the industry's dirty little secret, and the advertising executives have no intention of making this unrealistic trend in advertising imagery better known to the public than it already is. It's gotten so bad that even Julia Roberts isn't beautiful enough. In fact, L'Oreal ads featuring her in the U.K. were so unrealistic that the country's Advertising Standards Authority refused to allow them to run, saying that the ads falsified results.

The trouble is, *every* commercial image we now see is "unreal." But the unsuspecting consumer (that's us!) takes the images at face value, inviting ridiculous ideals of perfection into the subconscious. We form judgmental, unrealistic core beliefs about how we should be, and then stand in front of the mirror and hate our faces and bodies. We believe our sex lives aren't hot enough, our houses aren't big enough, and our kids aren't smart enough. Happiness, instead of being an internal condition that just *is* for no particular reason, suddenly becomes an elusive goal based on socially programmed expectations that have nothing to do with reality.

To fill the aching gap between our expectations and reality, we stuff ourselves with food, drugs, alcohol, and prescription medications—anything to take the pain away. We constantly distract ourselves with texting, Twitter, Facebook, cell phones, e-mails, voice mails, music, video games, radio, television, and social activities. The simple "here and now" is not enough, because we believe that *we* are not enough. And anything that takes us away from ourselves seems to be a good thing. Yet how can we possibly achieve or even desire the lucidity and empowerment of present-time consciousness when we're constantly striving to escape the present moment?

Mirror, Mirror on the Wall . . .

Are you happy with your body? Unhappy? What core beliefs do you hold about your physical image?

Strip down and stand in front of a full-length mirror. Notice what you focus on. What emotions do you feel as you simply observe your body? Anxiety? Vulnerability? Pain? Resentment? Self-hatred? Joy? Gratitude? Pleasure? Now ask yourself the truth question: "Would I ever choose to feel this way toward my body?"

If that brings a "Hell no!" then follow the rules for setting intentions by focusing on what your heart truly chooses to feel when it comes to a relationship with your body. Confident? Accepting? Delicious? Forgiving? Loving? Whatever word your heart expresses, now put it in the "I am" statement. Declare your "I am" statement out loud three times as you look in the mirror. For example, "I am delicious," "I am delicious," "I am delicious."

Now it's time to use your imagination to bridge the reactive emotions you have about your body with the relationship you are now consciously choosing to create. Allow the feeling to come to the surface as you imagine yourself in an "I am delicious" way. How does it feel to imagine it? Immediately a feeling, such as joy, will start to beat in your heart. You now have an intention: "I am delicious, feeling joyful."

Now we want to run the See Feel Hear Challenge. Reconnect to the emotion that was triggered by your looking at your naked body in the mirror. Put your hand in the "I love you" gesture over your heart and say, "Infinite Love & Gratitude." Fill yourself with Infinite Love & Gratitude.

See the thoughts, memories, and images that come from looking at yourself in the mirror. Say, "Infinite Love & Gratitude." *Feel* what it feels like to be in your body as you look at yourself naked in the mirror. Say again, "Infinite Love & Gratitude." *Hear* the voice of your body inside your mind. Hear what it's saying to you. As you do this, say, "Infinite Love & Gratitude."

Now focus upon the intention you have created—for example, "I am delicious, feeling joyful"—and connect with the emotion that the intention statement brings up. For example, the emotion may be *grateful* or even *shame.* Regardless of the emotion stemming from the intention, say, "Infinite Love & Gratitude." See your body with that emotion. Feel your body with that emotion. Hear your body with that emotion. Repeat, "Infinite Love & Gratitude."

SFH Pearl: Throughout the process, be sure you say "Infinite Love & Gratitude" until you notice a shift in what you are seeing, feeling, or hearing. Trust the process. Even if it's not happening right away, there will be a shift. In Chapter 11 we'll take you even deeper into the See Feel Hear Challenge when we address addiction and a part of the Challenge known as the *black hole.*

Changing Places

"The past gives you an identity, and the future holds the promise of salvation, of fulfillment in whatever form," writes Eckhart Tolle. "Both are illusions."[2]

The past might be an illusion, but humans are really good at basing their lives around it. One of the reasons why it's difficult to stay present in the now is because every thought we think—our whole identity—is based in past experiences. In every new situation, the brain immediately seeks familiar patterns from the past to help explain what's going on in the present. In fact, pattern recognition is one of the very first brain functions we use. Impressions are firing, and associations are linking neural networks in our brains every moment. This is why when we meet someone new, sometimes we perhaps think, *Wow, you look so much like my friend Tim!* Or we're learning a new e-mail system and think it's "like" Thunderbird. Or we're watching clouds and see the shapes of birds and lamp shades float by.

Everything we experience is filtered through the neurological network of what's already known, giving us "reality." So, do we ever really see, feel, and hear the truth of what's happening around us? No—not unless we learn how to access the present moment in its fullness and consciously evolve the old associations and thoughts with intention.

In every moment, we're either asleep, unconsciously being the sum total of what we've been, or awake to the sum total of what we consciously are now. And it's in the powerful state of present-time consciousness that we can most effectively mold what we are now into whatever we want to become by using the power of imagination.

Scientists now realize that the brain and body can't tell the difference between physical reality and imaging a different reality. At the Lerner Research Institute, the biomedical engineering department of the Cleveland Clinic, tests were conducted to see whether mental training could create significant muscle-strength increases in little-finger muscles and elbow-flexor muscles. Two groups of healthy volunteers mentally exercised their little fingers and their elbow muscles 5 days a week for 15 minutes over a 12-week span. A control group did no exercises, and a fourth group performed the actual physical exercises over the same time period for the same duration.

The results astounded researchers. It came as no surprise that those who did the physical training increased their muscle strength by 53 percent. As for those who did the mental training, the elbow-muscle group increased their strength by 13.5 percent, and the little-finger group increased their muscle strength by 35 percent![3] So what does this mean for you?

When you do the See Feel Hear Challenge, you set your intention on whatever emotional state and situation you desire to experience. Then you use your imagination to conjure the scene and all the sensory information: the smells, the taste, the touch, and the sounds. You literally place yourself where and how you want to be in your mind's eye, and your brain does the rest. Neurons fire, synapses connect, and neurotransmitters aligned with the emotions you're evoking through your visualization are released into the body.[1] And guess what? Your body responds!

You feel lighter, happier. From the safety of your conscious intention, you process all the subconscious messages, visuals, and feelings that come up; all the inner conversations, fears, and perceived blocks that seem to be standing in the way of your dreams. In your imagination, you begin to experience the desired state of mind and emotion more deeply. The chemicals shift and cascade in your brain and body, sending out matching electromagnetic frequencies into the quantum field that say, "Hey! This is really who I am! This is what I'm equal to! Bring it on!" And just like the people who strengthened their pinky fingers with their minds alone, your body and situations in life start to change.

Is it easy? Absolutely! Are there challenges to change? Absolutely! And one of the most insidious challenges is the chronic dissatisfaction with the now that sabotages our lives. Instead of loving what we are and imagining what we can be, we dwell on what we hate and don't want! But, as we wake up to how the world programs us into states of discontent, that changes, too. It's all just part of the amazing journey that happens when we decide to pick up the reins of responsibility and drive the dream where we want to go—awake and excited instead of nodding off or snoozing at the wheel.

Touching Present-Time Consciousness

Take a few moments to consider the various ways in which you avoid being present in your life. Does your cell phone never leave your grasp? Are you texting as you drift off to sleep? Is the radio or iPod constantly filling your ears with music? Do you seek out constant company, even when you don't feel like being around others?

Stop whatever you're doing and choose to take 15 minutes to be alone, with no stimulation, and do absolutely nothing. Just breathe and be.

What was your experience? Did you feel stress? Nervousness? Irritation? Frustration? Or peace, calm, and comfort? Run a See Feel Hear Challenge on your reaction.

❤

Chapter 8

The Mind as a Tormentor

*"The dark thought, the shame, the malice,
meet them at the door laughing and invite them in.
Be grateful for whoever comes, because each
has been sent as a guide from beyond."*

— RUMI[1]

In the now of present-time consciousness, you're comfortable in your skin. The mind is at peace while you're *being* what and where you are in the moment. Whether it's making love, standing in line at the grocery store, or sitting in the dentist's chair getting your teeth cleaned, there's no struggle against the moment, no wanting to be elsewhere, no discontent—you're simply the observer.

The number one thing that switches you out of PTC and a state of peaceful, vibrant awareness is judgment. "I'd rather be digging ditches in Antarctica in my underwear than have this woman digging in my mouth!" your mind screams as your dental appointment drags past. Of course, if you were in Antarctica, your mind would be screaming about wanting to be on a tropical beach somewhere. But the point is, by assessing any experience as good or bad, right or wrong, you instantly move out of present-time consciousness and trigger resistance that irritates your mind, body, and emotions.

> I was leading a client through the See Feel Hear Challenge, and the process took us through several rounds into a black hole. On the third loop through, as she saw images around the emotion of receiving, she instantly broke into tears. Later she revealed that for 25 years she'd harbored resentment and anger toward her father, and that for the last two years of his life she hadn't spoken to him once. During the See Feel Hear Challenge, she received images of him, embraced him fully with all her heart, and experienced a colossal shift! To witness this was, for me, an honor of the highest order.
>
> — Ed S.

Your heart and brain rhythms become irregular and choppy. The body responds with a shift in pH to a more acidic state. Synapses fire in the brain, cortisol is released, and the body enters a stressful fight-or-flight mode. Digestion shuts down, and the latte you drank before getting to the dentist's office curdles in your stomach. A headache develops. And these are just the immediate, short-term results of losing track of the now. What happens when this becomes a conditioned state over the course of a lifetime? What's the ripple effect?

A Polarized World

Assessment is critical to survival. The neighbor's normally locked-up pit bull stands in the driveway between you and your car, and you must instantly discern the danger level. You pull into the passing lane, determining that an oncoming car is far enough away to pass safely. But unless you become present with your thoughts and emotions, necessary discernment easily morphs into unhealthy judgment. Why? Because as human beings, we perceive reality through the lens of opposites.

Polarity is the primal foundation of mass. Within seconds after the big bang, positive and negative were born in the form of positrons and electrons. These oppositely charged particles soon coalesced into atoms, becoming hydrogen and other hot gases. Over billions of years, they cooled and condensed into matter; and galaxies, stars, planets, and then life forms were born.

Our very first moment in this world is spent screaming in reaction to differences! The harsh, dry coldness of a well-lit delivery room is the complete opposite of the darkly soothing, warm amniotic waters we floated in for nine months. And that's just the start! Immediately, our senses begin informing us that Mama's skin is smooth and Papa's is rough. Her voice is soft and high, and his is grumbly and deep. Apple juice tastes good, and spinach tastes bad. Quickly we learn left from right, big from small, back from front. We also learn that pooping in the potty is the right thing to do and that finger painting with body waste is wrong.

We grow up to be fat and skinny, blond and brunette, tall and short; and depending upon social norms, one state is always judged as being better than the other. Our emotions shift from happy to sad, anxious to peaceful, angry to kind depending on our judgment of what's happening in the moment, triggering synapses in the brain to release neuropeptides to match the frequency of our reactions.[2]

We bounce all over the map emotionally, and then we compound things by reacting to the emotions we're experiencing. We want to be happy, but with so much unassimilated subconscious material being triggered all the time, we often end up in negative spirals of emotion that are anything but happy.

Let's use Heather as an example. She gets an e-mail from an angry customer at work, and it shocks her system. Her immediate reaction is anger, and her brain instantly releases the neuropeptides of anger. She manages a civil reply. It's business after all. But after she hits SEND, her body is still bathed in the molecules of anger, and her mind responds to the emotions lingering in the body. *What a jerk!* she thinks. Her brain responds to the angry thought and releases more anger chemicals. She feels it and mentally reacts, seething. The brain obligingly releases more chemicals keyed to anger. By the end of the day, Heather's mind and body have cycled through a feedback loop that has her in an emotional storm.

A subconscious program that says, "When it hurts, go have a drink" kicks in. She heads to the nearest bar after work and drowns her emotions in alcohol. The next morning, she wakes up to a hangover and guilt, starting the day with more angry thoughts about herself and how helpless she feels in the face of life. She may not even remember what started the emotional spinout in the first place, but its effects might linger for days. And don't you know that the person who sent her the e-mail undoubtedly has the same kind of powerful programs running his or her show?

Like attracts like. Depending upon our emotional and mental state, we always draw to ourselves people and circumstances of matching frequency.

Gotcha!

When was the last time something or somebody really ticked you off? Or hurt you? Or made you anxious and upset? If you can, recall the details. Did it start off as something small and then escalate? Were you gnawing at what happened for days, feeling worse and worse?

Is this a recurring situation and feeling? Is there a pattern to what triggers you?

Ask yourself the truth question. Given a choice, would you choose this kind of experience? Hell no!? Then take this gift in strange wrapping paper and run the See Feel Hear Challenge on this emotional "gotcha!"

Neurons and the Karmic Wheel

In the West, karma is understood as a process of "As ye sow, so shall ye reap." If you put anger "out there," it will come back at you full force. But there's a more scientific and subtle view of karmic processes called *Hebbian learning.*

Take the previous example. The more Heather has angry thoughts or emotions, the more she has angry thoughts or emotions. Her thoughts and feelings don't change; *they simply become amplified.* It actually becomes easier and easier for her to have those thoughts, because as neuroscience has now shown, the more repetitive the thought, the more dense and efficient the neural pathways in the brain that fire those particular thoughts become. Commonly referred to as *Hebb's law,* this process is popularly summed up as, "Neurons that fire together wire together," creating a neurological network that is associated with specific thoughts and emotions.

Repetitive, anger-inducing thoughts such as *People are always taking advantage of me* and *I hate fielding complaints!* are linked through anger. If we could peer into Heather's brain, we'd find lots of neural pathways and connections with receptor sites designed to receive neurotransmitters chemically aligned to this one emotion. For example, her neural pathways of anger would look like a superhighway compared to her barely trod footpath of a neural pathway conducting love! Over time, these well-used paths become "hardwired" in her brain. The neurons become so accustomed to receiving anger chemicals that they can't receive any other kinds of neurotransmitters, such as those coded for joy or contentment.

Here lies the physiological foundation for karma.

Heather the office worker is now "destined" to have anger-inducing experiences. She can't help it! Her uncontrolled and repetitious angry thoughts and feelings have carved a superhighway in her brain. She's wired big-time to send and receive anger-based signals. She's trapped with her brain playing one "He done me wrong" country tune on a repeating loop that she can't escape. Will her fated destination be the one that she wants? Hardly!

The Lies Inside Our Heads

The thoughts that repeat themselves over and over are rarely the "good" thoughts. It's much easier to believe *I don't deserve love* than *I'm worthy of love and affection.* Why? Because negative input from the environment carries more emotional impact than positive input. Getting a gold star on your homework from the teacher just doesn't have the same punch as being humiliated in front of the whole class for a wrong answer. Your father's praise for your raking of the lawn can't compete with the shouting match and spanking you got for being a "no-good, little liar"!

The embarrassment, indignation, anger, shame, and other emotions from such events release powerful chemicals that can create a firestorm in our brains and bodies. We easily get overloaded. And the effects can last for days! The resulting "negative" imprinting in our psyches is extremely potent. Without conscious tools, strategies, or support to process the experiences and the emotions, the critical voice—whether it belonged to a parent, teacher, friend, or another relative—remains embedded in the subconscious. The disapproving words echo for decades, becoming the basis for the self-judgments and lies we believe about ourselves that are contrary to our true state of being as spirits of pure love.

To make matters worse, we're taught that thinking well of ourselves is immodest and even a sin! The end result is a bunch of negative self-talk that only proliferates as we grow older. Remember, "neurons that fire together wire together." As the neural pathways connected to our negative thought patterns and emotions strengthen and get more efficient, we come to have as little control over them as we do the other addictions we develop to drown out those ugly voices. Food, drugs, alcohol, sex, work, money, gambling—seeking relief, we get hooked on these things as well. Then we add fuel to the fire by judging ourselves as bad and wrong for doing so.

The Impact of Future Thinking

Logic dictates that if the now of present-time consciousness contains everything, the future must contain nothing. In fact, aside from a concept in our heads, it doesn't even exist. "People like us, who believe in physics, know that the distinction between past, present, and future is only a stubbornly persistent illusion," said Albert Einstein. "The only reason for time is so that everything doesn't happen at once."

The illusory future is responsible for one major tormentor: worry.

Yes, it's wise and practical to plan ahead. But there's absolutely no certainty that the future you plan for, strive for, and worry over will ever arrive—or you along with it. So you might as well tie your camel to the hitching post and walk away. In other words, set your intention in the direction of your heart's desire, use your imagination to bring up a feeling, take action according to the feeling of your heart's desire, do your best, and then let it go. What use is it to lie awake in bed at night worrying about whether things will turn out the way you want?

Remember, the now contains every possible state of mind or emotion you could ever choose. If you've already experienced the happiness of your intention, if you've already experienced the joy of having your dreams come true just by being present and imagining them, then haven't you already obtained your heart's desire? And if you've already obtained your heart's desire and can access the joy of it any moment you choose, what's to worry about? Doesn't it make sense to continue to choose to feel that way instead of carving an interstate highway of worry in your brain?

Remember, the best assurance of a bright tomorrow is a pleasantly sunny today. But if you don't have a lifeline to joy, happiness, and contentment; if you can't truly see, feel, and hear what's present in your life and feel gratitude for the gifts, no matter how strange their wrapping paper; if you're unaware of the emotions and thoughts running your life and you're stuck in the past and future with all the regrets, anxieties, and voices that come with those illusions, your karma is assured. And it's not the future you'd ever choose!

Fortunately, as you've discovered, changing your now is actually a very simple process. And destiny is just a series of nows shaped the way you want by your living with intention. Once you start using the See Feel Hear Challenge to process old, unassimilated emotions and imagine *being* your intentions in present-time consciousness, the "future" takes care of itself.

Where Does Your Mind Go?

What do you think about? What's the running conversation in your head as you're showering in the morning? Driving to work? Lying in bed at night? Are you present to what's going on? Or are you elsewhere, thinking about bills, the carpool schedule, or last night's reality-TV show?

Get in the habit of checking in with yourself. Program your wristwatch to give you an occasional "Where's my mind?" check. It's amazing to realize how little time we actually spend in present-time consciousness!

Once you remember to tune in, spend some time simply being aware of your surroundings. Take in the colors and sounds. Turn off the radio and unhook from the iPod for a little while. Sense your fingers gripping the steering wheel as you drive. Notice the people around you in the grocery store. Notice your breath. Notice your body. Notice your emotions. Notice the sunset. Notice how most people don't seem to be noticing.

It's okay if the mind chatters through all this. Just notice that, too. Notice where your mind wants to go and ask yourself, "Do I really want to go there?" Remember, you do have a choice in the matter!

Chapter 9

Responsibility and the Freedom to Choose

"You are song, a wished-for song.
Go through the ear to the center,
where the sky is, where wind,
where silent knowing.

Put seeds and cover them.
Blades will sprout
where you do your work."

— RUMI [1]

American journalist Sydney Harris once wrote, "We have not passed that subtle line between childhood and adulthood until we have stopped saying 'It got lost,' and say, 'I lost it.'" But really, how easy is it to pass that line? If you're like most people, it's not easy at all.

It takes courage to face the teacher and say that we didn't do our homework, knowing that we went to the movies instead. It takes guts to tell our parents that we left our new iPhone on the bus or admit to the boss that we made an accounting error on the company's tax returns. It takes guts to tell our husband or wife that we're not in love anymore. It takes guts, because in our minds, taking responsibility means taking the blame, and taking the blame means getting punished. And we all have powerfully painful associative memories squirreled away in our subconscious about that!

Just thinking about confessing our perceived wrongdoings makes our hearts race and our stomachs do flip-flops. How infinitely safer to blame the dog for eating your book report! How diverting to say somebody stole your phone and that another accountant got the figures wrong. How much safer it is to stay in a relationship because it's comfortable. Say anything, blame anybody; just don't be honest and get punished. If you're convincing and desperate enough, you might even end up believing your own story!

Self-Esteem and the Ego

We all want to feel good about ourselves. But which self are we concerned with feeling good about? Is it the image we hold of ourselves, or something deeper and more substantial?

The image, or persona, is all the things we think we are: spiritual person, intellectual, jock, femme fatale, fashion leader, Green Peace activist. These roles become the entirety of who we believe ourselves to be. As such, we're deeply invested in these images, and we'll go to great extremes to make sure they remain untarnished. The intellectual caught with a romance novel shoved in her purse lies: "Oh that? A friend left it in my car. Unbelievable the trash she reads!" The Green Peace activist with a Styrofoam container of leftovers on his desk protests, "Can you believe it? My last client ordered takeout, and I had to eat it out of *that!*"

We have a vested interest in being seen as consistent within the identities we create for ourselves. We definitely don't want to feel as if we're falling short or being seen as such. But the thing is, falling short is an inevitable part of being human. We all miss the mark occasionally—sometimes frequently! And the only way we can truly improve ourselves is to accept both the good sides and the perceived bad sides of ourselves, knowing it all can be changed.

Unfortunately, the world has created some pretty unreasonable standards for us to live up to. Western females must be thin, gorgeous, great cooks, good mothers, successful businesspeople, demure enough for the in-laws, and sexually uninhibited enough to keep their men satisfied. Males have to be great providers, manly enough to make their women feel safe and loved, and able to wipe out the competition in a hostile corporate takeover yet sensitive, emotionally available, and willing to change diapers. Above all, both sexes must have the money that buys the houses, the cars, and all the toys that spell success. Oh yes, and don't forget to vote—and pay your taxes.

One day my nine-year-old daughter came home from school with a severe stomachache. I had her lie on the sofa as I asked her what emotion her stomach was feeling, and she said, "Sad." I had her see, feel, and hear the sadness her tummy was feeling. When we got to hearing the sad voice, I asked her what the voice said, and she cried, "There's so much pressure to be perfect!" I asked her how that made her feel, to which she replied, "Frustrated, Mommy!" I guided her to see, feel, and hear that frustration. When we got to "hear," she heard a voice yelling at the teachers. It made her feel "happy" to release the frustration in her imagination, so we next digested "happy" by imagining that she was hugging her teachers, her classmates, and all the kids at school. She'd started the See Feel Hear Challenge while lying in a fetal position. By the end, her body was completely relaxed, her face was beaming with happiness, and the stomach pain was completely gone. We went on to talk about the ways that she can choose an intention when the sad or frustrated feelings come up again. What a gift to be able to guide my child through this process! For this, I am eternally grateful.

— Ann W.

Children start training in kindergarten to take responsibility for these ridiculous expectations: competing to get into the best grade schools so that they can get into the best colleges in order to obtain the best jobs that will enable them to have what they're supposed to have. They read magazines, watch TV shows, and play video games, absorbing the aggressive, sexualized images that teach them who they're supposed to grow up to be. And there's no margin for error. Never mind that perfection is only obtainable through Photoshop; it's expected nonetheless. Is it any wonder that people end up stressed, willing to do anything—beg, borrow, lie, cheat, steal, outsource, invade other nations, and destroy the environment—to make it happen?

Basing self-esteem upon our ability to take responsibility for maintaining unrealistic, socially fabricated core beliefs about how we're supposed to appear in the world is a recipe for personal and social disaster. And we do it all the time.

A Different Take on Responsibility

As little children, we're told not to be selfish. We're trained to think of others before ourselves. We're taught to be responsible, first and foremost, for living up to familial and then societal expectations. But how can we be responsible for anything if we've never learned to be responsible to ourselves? And what does being responsible to self even mean?

Making decisions grounded in our innermost integrity, choosing paths guided by our deepest truth, is not something we're shown how to do. Instead, we're taught to always depend upon externals and other people's rules and opinions for our choices. As a result, we consistently find ourselves in life situations that aren't fulfilling: in jobs we hate, with partners we don't love, buying things we don't need. Our souls ache, and we stuff our real emotions away; put our images on parade; and self-medicate with drugs, sex, and alcohol to ease the pain.

We subconsciously punish ourselves for our dishonesty. Forgetting that our bodies are divine temples, we starve them, sexualize them, and fill them with overly processed junk foods. We subject our minds to television, violent video games, rage music, and pornography. With no authentic outlets, we become angry and reactive, lashing out at life and people. In this space, there's no considering the needs of others or concern for their well-being. We hurt too much to care about others! How can life *not* hurt when it's all about serving a self that isn't even who we really are?

"Between stimulus and response is our greatest power, the freedom to choose," said educator and motivational speaker Stephen Covey. But until we dive inward to discover the beautiful, naturally loving, whole beings that we really are, we have no choice but to continue reacting to life. There can be no response, because response is a subtle, sensitive dance that's done from our hearts. Without response from the real self, there can be no freedom to choose.

Slowing Down to See, Feel, and Hear

The ego you've been taught to be responsible to, the "gotta look good at all costs" persona that's racing to keep it all together, is not the part of you that's going to be comfortable admitting that there are things that need addressing in your life, aspects of yourself that need improving, health considerations to deal with. This is not the part of you that's going to be comfortable doing the See Feel Hear Challenge. In fact, it's the part of you that won't want to do it at all.

"Things aren't *that* bad," the ego rationalizes. "Besides, I don't have *time* to sit and reflect on my problems and feelings. I don't have time to figure out what every little ache and pain means. They'll probably go away."

It's easy to dismiss the things that really matter when you don't know how to take your true feelings into consideration. We're taught to not care for ourselves, remember? You dearly want to study music, but you take accounting to please Daddy. You yearn for a few days' break at the beach, but spend your vacation repainting the house. Your heart aches at seeing a young panhandler on the street, and you long to give. But you clutch your wallet and walk past. You sense that there's something wrong with Aunt Jane, but you don't call her, only to later discover that she's had a stroke. You sense that there's something wrong with your heart, but you pop antacids and tell no one.

We've learned to ignore all the things that matter most. And thus we've lost the ability to make wise and fruitful choices.

Our feelings are our best guide through life. They tell us what the most fulfilling path is. They reveal what our souls want to experience. They act as early-warning systems for our health and give us silent messages about others that we need to hear and pay attention to. Using the See Feel Hear Challenge to develop our abilities to sense this kind of information via our inner vision— through our emotions and intuition, through listening to our bodies and learning to hear the "still, small voice within"—is one of the most responsible actions we can take. It makes us *response-able!*

In taking the time to care for ourselves and process our emotions, by slowing down and sensing inner information, we open ourselves to other sensory delights. We really *see* our children's joy in a new toy and stop what we're doing to play with them, opening ourselves to experience their joy. Maybe we don't go on that beach vacation, but the sunset stops us in our tracks for a few moments of breathless wonder and gratitude for life as we're carrying the paint cans to the garage.

We become aware of new possibilities and opportunities that we might otherwise miss while racing down the road to nowhere. Our friendships deepen. Our marriages and partnerships become more satisfying. We identify more fully with others' fears and woes, small victories and hopes. We connect in a greater variety of ways, becoming more compassionate and understanding. Life begins to flow, presenting fewer and fewer bumps and stresses. Time expands, and life becomes worth living. As we go deeper into our hearts, the world becomes beautiful, and our journey takes on the luster of a grand adventure.

And then one fine morning, we wake up and look around, surprised and pleased to discover that we're actually in the place where we've longed to be all along.

Who Do You Think You Are?

Where is your identity most invested? As a good parent? A great breadwinner? A faultless computer programmer? A flawless beauty? A good lover? Is this where your self-esteem and self-worth lie?

It's okay. We all soak up ideas of what and how we're supposed to be from other people, whether our parents or society. Then we take responsibility for being what we think we're supposed to be, rather than what and how we really are in our hearts and souls.

Contemplate the roles you play. Which ones feel good, and which ones don't? Which ones fit, and which ones don't? Is living up to these roles a source of pressure and anxiety?

What voices are in your head, telling you how to be, what to do, and what to not do? Are you "too cool" to do the See Feel Hear Challenge? Too busy? These, too, are identities that keep us from being the authentic selves we long to be.

Chapter 10

Social Conditioning

"Why do you stay in prison
when the door is so wide open?

Move outside the tangle of fear-thinking.
Live in silence."

— R U M I [1]

We like to think of ourselves as free agents, independently creating our own destiny. We are free agents—in theory. And we do create our own destiny. It's just that the destiny we're creating is mostly shaped by external influences so subtle and intricately interwoven that we're not aware of them. Remember the guy who ended up as a pest controller because of one traumatic event when he was two years old, an event he didn't even remember? Well, that's nothing in comparison to the total-immersion influence of social conditioning!

We absorb the beliefs, habits, preferences, and prejudices of our parents, teachers, and religious leaders without even knowing we're doing it. Seventy-one percent of U.S. teens will follow in their parents' ideological footsteps, voting Republican or Democratic as their parents voted. Fifty-nine percent will end up embracing their parents' religions or lack of one for the rest of their lives.[2] We're taught to clean our plates because children are starving in Africa; do things because an adult says so; confuse platitudes with truth; and wonder if indeed we really would "jump off a bridge" if our friends were doing it, just as our parents said we would.

Despite the desire to stand out, we also subconsciously believe that there's safety in numbers. Herd consciousness is in our genes, and there's a strong survival pull to do what everybody else does. Also known as "being popular," this need to conform is similar to being an impala grazing on the African veld. If we can lose ourselves in the crowd, there are fewer chances of getting attacked. But conforming can also get us into hot water, and many people have the tattoos and nose rings to prove it! And just in case you doubt the power of mob mentality, go to a rock concert for a direct experience of the power of the group mind. Shrieking and singing along with the band, you wave your cell phone in the air, suddenly at one with the strangers pressing around you—a wonderful, exciting, and at times scary experience!

A Common Bond

We resonate to our environment. Our hearts beat synchronously with the Schumann resonances, the extremely low frequencies of the Earth's electromagnetic field. We share a consensus reality with our countrymen, unquestioningly believing certain things about ourselves. Jews in Israel share a strong ethnic bond of pain and suffering. Americans still believe they're the world's heroes 67 years after being the only nation on Earth to use atomic bombs against another country's citizenry.

We're constantly subject to subtly agreed-upon information fields, and we subconsciously adopt these multiple influences as part of our identity. Missourians share a belief in their statewide stubbornness. Alaskans are rugged individualists. We share loyalties to the cities we live in and our local sports teams, and we identify with our schools, churches, synagogues, mosques, and Moose Lodges. All this information affects our self-image, how we relate to others, the words we use to communicate, the careers we choose, the clothes we wear, even the beer we drink. And we don't even know it!

A Dangerous Harvest

Of all the psychological core beliefs that Westerners share, shame is probably the most destructive. An unrelenting sense of worthlessness, inadequacy, and feeling unwanted, it doesn't take much to trigger shame in this world. We miss a *Jeopardy!* question in front of our friends and feel stupid. Unable to crack the top on a jar of olives, we feel weak. Someone rolls past in a wheelchair, and we avert our eyes. God help us if someone calls our sexual prowess into question.

We glance in the mirror after showering and feel shame. A zit on the chin makes us want to hide in the closet. We watch the neighbor pull out of the garage in a new Porsche, and a year's worth of therapy goes *poof!* And once we are in the deep black hole of shame, we only see, feel, and hear what the subconscious program of the emotion allows us to perceive. It gets to the point where we dread being caught in a mistake of any kind, so we curtail our enthusiasm and sense of adventure, pulling into our protective shells. We adopt the label of shame and begin to identify ourselves with the reactive pattern itself, rather than seeing it as a messenger from a deeper part of ourselves that's now ready to grow and blossom.

The See Feel Hear Challenge has given me a deeper appreciation for the connection between emotions and the health of my body. I'm not so quick to ignore physical symptoms or the expression of emotions, and I'm now open, ready, willing, and able to discover what emotions might be trapped within any part of my body. I now know that we are all divinely and intelligently designed to heal, regenerate, and be whole.

— Betsy W.

At its core, shame is a spiritual dialogue. We look at life, inhale the vastness of the universe, and rightfully feel very small and insignificant in the scheme of things. Religion does nothing to help the situation with stories about God's displeasure with humanity and our general unworthiness. But even though it's spiritual at its foundations, thought and emotional patterns of shame have a destructive impact on the beating of our hearts, our brain chemistry, our hormonal cycles, and our digestion. In the moment of shame, we go through a "Hulk-like" metamorphosis where we become someone else in mind and body, and our health and all our relationships suffer accordingly.

The good news is, even though it's commonly thought that healing shame requires patience and the courage to uncover and explore the shaming events that created it, healing shame can occur quickly and in an extremely empowering and inspiring way. Just understanding that shame is a dialogue that your spirit wants to have with you, rather than a life sentence of misery, is a huge step in the right direction.

Transforming Shame

Now is the time to accept being you. Let's transform the wounds of childhood, embrace grief, and fill our hearts with love as we give a new voice to our inner child. Whether it's shame-bound feelings in your heart or overwhelming thoughts and feelings of anger, sadness, and fear—whether it's perceived issues around embracing your sexuality or fear of being in a relationship—stand up tall and look shame directly in the eyes.

Wherever you are right now, begin repeating, "Regardless of shame, I love myself and accept myself exactly as I am, who I am, and where I am in this moment. Infinite Love & Gratitude!"

Note the emotions that come up in response to this declaration. If you have time, immediately run the See Feel Hear Challenge. If necessary, do it later. Use the previous statement as your intent. Imagine how it feels to absolutely love yourself just as you are. Then engage shame. "Infinite Love & Gratitude to shame." What does shame look like? See the images and memories. "Infinite Love & Gratitude." Say it several times. How do the words affect your body? Where do you feel them? Is there another emotion attached? "Infinite Love & Gratitude" to whatever the next feeling or emotion is.

What do these images have to say? Hear the voices. "Infinite Love & Gratitude to _____." As you go through the various emotions that come up during the process, remember to set your intention. Self-love and acceptance are the antithesis of shame!

The Media

Just in case you weren't sure that you were totally lacking in beauty, brains, ability, and an adequate lifestyle, there's always the entertainment media to convince you of your inferiority, and the advertising industry to convince you how to compensate for it. Corporations spent $144 billion on TV, radio, and print advertising in 2011, with over $12 billion aimed at hawking sugar-coated cereals, candy, toys, and violent video games to children under age 12.[3] In the U.S., people watch television an average of four hours per day. This means that by age 70, most people have spent over 14 years watching TV, four of which were spent watching commercials, with the average adult subjected to an average of 1,080 per week!

And get this: Studies show that watching TV puts your brain into a low alpha brain-wave state between 8 and 12 hertz, the same frequency state as meditation and hypnosis. In this light trance, we are highly suggestible, and messages imprint deeply. Advertisers know this and use functional magnetic resonance imaging (fMRI) to track blood flow in the brains of test subjects of all ages to discover which areas of the brain are most effectively impacted by visual and auditory cues. The science of neuromarketing ensures that every image and color, every word and sound used in ads, is deliberately chosen to create maximum emotional impact so that the deepest mental impression is made.

Maybe Ford doesn't have "a better idea," but if they can convince you they do, you'll be making payments on that car for a long time. And your selection will be a subtle advertisement, in turn influencing everybody who sees you drive by with the ongoing message, "Hey guys! Ford is the best. I put my money on it!" And it's not just our cars. Every time we buy something, we unwittingly become partners in the corporate sales game. We even proudly purchase and wear their billboards, sporting T-shirts and jackets with catchy brand slogans we identify with, such as Livestrong. And now look at Lance Armstrong.

It's hard to swallow, but if we're not conscious of why we make the choices we do, both big and small, the sad truth is that somebody *else* has done the deciding for us. This perhaps explains why America, which spent almost $140 billion in advertising in 2012 globally ranks 1st in obesity,[4] while ranking 33rd for the health of its citizens, behind Kuwait, South Korea, Cuba, and Slovenia.[5] Would anyone *consciously* choose obesity and poor health? Of course not! This begs the question, why are we so obese? And why are we supporting sickness care instead of health care? Are we hypnotized into buying bad health?

The average modern American consumes 150 pounds of sugar and 183 pounds of meat a year. This is far removed from the simple diets we were eating as a nation just 50 years ago. Would we be eating so differently now if we weren't constantly being sold on the products so conveniently packaged for us? Would over 90 percent of seniors in the United States and 58 percent of nonelderly adults rely on prescription medicine on a regular basis if the big pharmaceutical companies weren't spending over $5 billion per year on direct-to-consumer advertising that tells us what pills we can't live without? And would we still take them if we knew that these same "safe" pills kill over 106,000 Americans and hospitalize over 2 million others every year due to adverse effects of properly administered, FDA-approved drugs?[6]

The Road Less Traveled

We're constantly being told who we "should" be and what we "should" want. Is it any wonder that the last voice we can hear in our heads is our own? We're socially conditioned to believe in our government officials and Excedrin. But trust ourselves? Trust subtle feelings and intuition? Trust the still, small voice within? Nobody tells us to do that!

This is why it's so easy to dismiss the messages when we do get them. We're also not accustomed to subtlety. The media bombards us with screaming neon colors, flashing billboards, and shouted statements about "*super*-hydrating *maxi*-polishing *activators!*" Fanfare music that should attend the Second Coming, not a commercial for furniture polish, blares in the background. Is it any wonder that we feel hesitant engaging something like the See Feel Hear Challenge, which focuses us on learning the simple language of inner vision, sensing, and hearing?

It's a lot easier to go buy a wonder drug.

But if we train ourselves to take the time to quietly go within to see, feel, and hear what our bodies and emotions are telling us, we can discern our own voices from the medley of noise around us. We naturally rise above the impact of social conditioning. By recovering our ability to discern our genuine needs and desires, reestablishing a connection with body and soul, we become our own guides and teachers. As we trust ourselves more and more, our potentials begin to flower. Leaving the refuge of sameness, we have more to live for, more to experience, and more to give.

Chapter 11

Dialoguing with Addiction

"When water gets caught in habitual whirlpools, dig a way out through the bottom to the ocean. There is a secret medicine given only to those who hurt so hard they can't hope."

— R U M I [1]

The Cadillac of gifts in strange wrapping paper, addiction comes in a wide variety of models. Whether it's chronic emotions or stress, alcohol or drugs, TV or Facebook, video games, cigarettes, success, hypochondria, or youthfulness, addictions are huge red flags pointing us in the direction of our personal awakening. They reflect our perceived greatest weaknesses that, once addressed, can become our greatest strengths.

But first we have to dive beneath addiction's mask.

It's not the addiction itself that's important, but rather what it's being used to hide. Addictions are always diversion techniques, and, like every other "dis-ease," addiction has its own voice of protection. What wounds lie unseen? What messages bide their time deep inside the subconscious, bursting to come out; ready to be seen, felt, and heard through the See Feel Hear dialogue; waiting to be turned into wisdom so that you can experience a whole new way of living?

The Face of Addiction

According to the American Society for Addiction Medicine, addiction is "a primary, chronic disease of brain reward, motivation, memory, and related circuitry. . . . Addiction is characterized by inability to consistently abstain, impairment in behavioral control, craving, diminished recognition of significant problems with one's behaviors and interpersonal relationships, and a dysfunctional emotional response."[2]

Everyone is addicted to something, even if it's just core beliefs. Substance abuse is considered almost normal nowadays. An estimated 22.6 million Americans age 12 and up use illicit drugs, an eight percent increase since 2002. Over half of Americans age 12 and older drink alcohol.[3] How do we get hooked? Where do addictions, obsessive-compulsive thoughts, feelings, words, and relationships come from? Why is it so difficult to break the patterns of use and abuse?

Most people don't start life as addicts. But have you ever noticed how easy it is to get into a habit? We take the same routes to the grocery store. Our thoughts constantly cycle through the same story lines and perceived problems. We watch the same TV shows and wear the same styles of clothing for years. We can even make a habit of using the same bathroom stall at work. It's human nature to take comfort in known routines and to adopt certain behaviors. When we do something that the body considers even mildly pleasurable, which can also translate as "safe," chemical signals traverse the mesolimbic pathway to the nucleus accumbens, which releases dopamine neurotransmitters.

A neural-learning device that positively reinforces us to adopt certain behaviors, such as eating and mating to ensure survival of the species, the release of dopamine and other brain chemicals gives us a feel-good moment that prompts us to repeat the action. Eat that first banana, and the reward center kicks in. Eat bitter berries and spend the night sick in the bushes, and your brain sends different signals down a different pathway, reminding you never to go there again.

As psychoneuroimmunologist Dr. Candace Pert puts it, "The very highest, most intelligent part of our brain is drenched in receptors to make us use pleasure as a criterion for our decisions."[4] The trouble is, in our search for pleasure from sources *outside us,* we can overdo a good thing. Whether it's too many bananas or too much sex or Valium, after a while the brain's reward system becomes overstimulated, and it takes ever-increasing amounts of the desired substance or action for the brain to release enough dopamine to give us the same high and level of comfort. Because the brain areas involved regulate emotions, cognition, motivation, and pleasure, all these things get mixed up, resulting in an illogical, unhealthy, compulsive striving to attain the source of stimulation over and over again.

Emotional Addiction

"The striking pattern of neuropeptide receptor distribution in mood-regulating areas of the brain, as well as their role in mediating communication through the whole organism, makes neuropeptides the obvious candidates for the biochemical mediation of emotion,"[5] says Dr. Pert. Former chief of brain biochemistry of the Clinical Neuroscience Branch at the National Institute of Mental Health and discoverer of what are now called the "molecules of emotion," Pert believes that "emotions orchestrate the interactions among all our organs and systems," triggering an electromagnetic frequency that is emanated by the body; a frequency that other people can sense and "read."[6]

It's almost as if the body were wired to get hooked on emotions. They run the show. Unfortunately, if we repeat a specific emotion over and over, receptor sites can get hooked on the neuropeptide vibrating to that emotion. And we don't even have to repeat the same triggering action to get the emotional hit that we come to crave. Because the brain and body are unable to tell the difference between a situation that's physically occurring in the now and the memory of it, all we have to do is repeat memories of the original incident to get the same chemical release. Eventually our neurons become so addicted to whatever emotion is consistently being triggered that even memories are no longer needed. A gap develops between the conscious and subconscious minds. Anger, anxiety, and depression become our constant reality, and we begin to think in ways that stimulate more and more production of the needed neuropeptide. We haven't got a clue that a subconscious addictive loop has been set into motion between mind and body, and that the frequency that we now emanate causes us to attract relationships and circumstances to feed this emotional addiction.

> The See Feel Hear Challenge enables my clients to climb the highest mountains of their lives, regardless of how hard their lives are at that moment. They are always amazed by the incredible shifts they experience through the process.
>
> — Charles M.

Brain Change

Fortunately, neurophysiologists have discovered that the brain is a highly adaptive organ that changes throughout our lives. Far from the old model of "brain freeze," which viewed the brain as incapable of changing after young adulthood, scientists now know about *neuroplasticity,* the ability of our brains to continue creating new neural networks in response to different information input. The brain can even create new information networks to compensate for areas of the brain that have been damaged or surgically removed, restoring critical cognitive and motor functions to people at any age.

This is wonderful news for people who are experiencing addiction.

Yes, addiction creates vast neural superhighways in the brain. It may damage the mesolimbic area and inhibit judgment and critical thinking. It may inhibit the brain's ability to receive peptides and neurotransmitters that aren't linked to the addiction. But we can change all of this by sincerely embracing the desire for healing and then taking action. Despite much literature to the contrary, there is a high rate of recovery among *untreated* alcoholics and addicts. An estimated 40 percent of all alcoholics get sober without intervention. The majority of heroin addicts break the habit in 11 years (if they survive that long), also on their own.[7] Regardless of the patterns of addiction and all of the accompanying physical, emotional, and mental impacts, these people were still capable of making a decision. And once they made a choice to change, they changed.

Every addiction and every emotional pattern that drives addiction has only a certain amount of fuel. Eventually they all run out of reactive momentum. As stated before, the subconscious mind's purpose is to protect us in the moment. Each time the programs of protection are activated, their emotional potential, or "charge," diminishes. At some point, there will be a crescendo, a time or an event where the addict has "had enough" and a shift occurs. Unfortunately, until the addiction plays out and the individual finally arrives at his or her personal rock-bottom place, where either change or death must occur, entire lives are wrecked by the repeating patterns of abuse.

Understanding the dynamics involved in addiction, whether emotional addiction or otherwise, helps us reframe the perceptions we have toward the addictive cycle. Understanding takes us a little way into the observer mode, giving us a tiny toehold on the thing that we perceive has got us by the throat. And the See Feel Hear Challenge is a great tool for getting to the root emotional patterns of addiction and for beginning the process of rewiring the brain into harmonious and conscious patterns.

Pick Your Poison

Infinite Love & Gratitude to addictions. We all experience them. Here's an opportunity to take an honest look at yourself—not righting or wronging yourself, not shaming yourself—but rather acknowledging the addict that's speaking through and to you right now. And if you're shaming and blaming and guilting yourself, Infinite Love & Gratitude to that as well. This is your new starting point.

Given a choice to create your life, a day, or a moment, would you ever choose to be an addict? Say it: "Hell no!" Say it out loud: *"Hell no!"*

Go into your heart right now and follow the two golden rules of manifesting intentions. What does your heart choose to feel? Write that feeling down on a piece of paper. Now put the words *I am* in front of that word or words, and say the intention out loud three times—for example, "I am whole, I am whole, I am whole." Place your hand in the "I love you" gesture over your heart.

Imagination is always necessary for setting an intention, but especially so when getting to the heart of the matter of addiction. How does it feel to imagine yourself in the land of "I am whole"? Write down that feeling. Let's say you feel happy. Now you have an intention statement: "I am whole, feeling happy."

Now, run the full three-prong SFH on the addiction that's speaking to you, the habit that's speaking *through* you, telling you to wake up and live your life with intention.

Note: This is highly emotional territory and not the place to take shortcuts. It would be a great idea to run the SFH associated with *all* the emotions that the addiction brings up, and don't be surprised if you run through many emotions.

A Pathway Through Addiction: The Black Hole

The obsessive patterns that come with addiction are relentless. Remember, the subconscious mind is reactive. By nature it's obsessive and compulsive. It's rather like HAL, the computer gone haywire in *2001: A Space Odyssey,* which only knows to carry out its programmed protection function: "I must protect. I must protect. I must protect . . ."

Stuck in a loop, the subconscious triggers whatever pain-reducing, protective activity the personality has selected: cutting, gambling, drinking, porn. There's no OFF switch to the pattern, and it will keep firing in the brain until the subconsciously perceived need to protect has been requited *at the level of the subconscious mind.* This is why it's almost impossible to simply and consciously say "No!" when we are in the throes of an addictive pattern. The subconscious original protection order has developed a mind of its own. It has grooved a veritable neuron superhighway in the brain, ensuring that the easiest path to take is always the path of the addiction.

The most effective evolutionary pathway out of addiction is *through* the addiction by consciously mirroring the obsessive action of the subconscious mind.

This is what the See Feel Hear Challenge does when you deliberately cycle into a black hole. Remember, every subconscious program, every OCD conversation, only has so much fuel. There's only so much information contained in the original triggering event that the subconscious is responding to with its protection-order program. Your dad only yelled so long that morning. He only said certain things that sliced so deep you couldn't handle them. Because the input is limited, the protection program created by your subconscious is also only so big.

If you can stay with the SFH process and cycle through the seemingly relentless series of negative voices, images, and feelings that surround an addiction, at some point the subconscious protection program will run out of steam. You'll have brought it all to the light of consciousness at last—or at least as much of it as your subconscious mind will permit in that particular moment. By repeatedly doing the See Feel Hear Challenge with the addiction, instead of experiencing the devastation of years of addiction before hitting rock bottom, you can actually induce the shift safely and manageably. It becomes a choice.

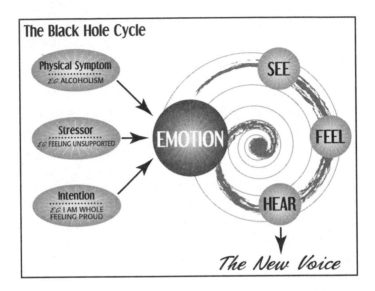

You'll know when you've reached the end of the black hole each time, because the voice inside finally says something more cheerful than, "You jerk!" It says something positive instead, like, "That's not true," "You're perfect exactly as you are," or "I love you." When this happens, you know you've reached HAL's core and assimilated all, or at least a substantial portion, of the subconscious reactive program running the addiction dialogue. Obsessions and compulsions are perfect territory for using the See Feel Hear Challenge and diving into black holes. At the end of the next section, we'll coach you through one!

A Dialogue with OCD

Obsessive-compulsive disorder (OCD) is characterized by obsessions or compulsions (or both) that are time-consuming or distressing, or that interfere with normal routines, relationships, and simple daily functioning. Obsessions are persistent ideas, images, or thoughts that intrude into a person's thinking, causing excessive worry and anxiety. Compulsions are mental acts or repetitive behaviors performed in response to obsessions to relieve or prevent worry or anxiety. They often have the intent of magically preventing or prompting avoidance of some dreaded event, such as death, illness, or some perceived misfortune.

The conversation of OCD has many faces, but the style and manner of the thoughts and behaviors presented by people so diagnosed are remarkable and unmistakably consistent.

The Faces of OCD

❧ *Checkers* feel compelled to repeatedly check objects, such as doors, locks, and the OFF settings on household appliances to feel assured that they've averted potential disasters.

❦ *Washers and Cleaners* have obsessions about the possibility of contamination by dirt, germs, viruses, or foreign substances.

❦ *Orderers and Repeaters* feel that they must arrange certain items in a particular, exact, "perfect" way, or they might repeat particular actions over and over.

❦ *Pure Obsessionals* experience unwanted, intrusive, horrific thoughts and images of causing danger or harm to others.

❦ *Hoarders* collect insignificant items and have difficulty throwing away things that most people would consider to be junk.

❦ *People with Scrupulosity* obsess about religious, ethical, or moral values; they wear a mask of always appearing as or attempting to be good.

Most people can identify with all of these faces of OCD to some extent. Who hasn't checked a second time to see whether the door was locked? And who hasn't occasionally let the magazines pile up to an unreasonable degree? It's only when behavior interferes with daily living that we know there's a deeper subconscious conversation at hand. It's important to observe all reactive thought patterns and behaviors as a meaningful dialogue and an opportunity to run the See Feel Hear Challenge. As a result of taking the observer role, you'll not only begin to notice changes in your thoughts and behaviors, but also feel connected and empowered to live in the present moment.

Riding a Black Hole

Compulsions are about control. Who or what are you obsessed with? Connect to the part of you that needs to alphabetize the soup cans in the cupboard, the part that battles germs by carrying baby wipes to clean off public door handles before touching them, the part that bites your nails until they bleed, the part that chronically checks the stove.

As you tune in to your own personal conversation with obsessive thoughts and compulsive behaviors, notice the emotion that comes up. Is it anxiety? Frustration? Helplessness? Shame? Anger? Panic? Allow yourself to appreciate the level of the emotion you're feeling that stems from the OCD conversation you're participating in.

Zero to ten, what do you rate that emotion? Would you ever choose to feel this way? Of course not! So now is the time to set an intention and guide this protective part of you into a new reality in which you are free to be authentic with whatever you choose, rather than being compelled to repeat actions when you're upset because you believe you have no choice. In other words, it's okay to organize your sock drawer by matching colors, and it's okay to stack the soup cans from *A* to *Z*—if that's what you really *want* to do rather than *have* to do because you have no conscious control over the situation.

Set an intention.

So what does your heart choose to feel? Listen to your heart and write this feeling down on a piece of paper. Whatever that feeling is, put the words *I am* in front of it and say the intention statement out loud three times with your hand in the "I love you" gesture over your heart.

Now acknowledge that you're open to using your imagination. Once you have done so, bring up the feeling that you experience as you imagine yourself in the mind, heart, and relationships of "I am _____, feeling _____" (whatever your intention is). Write that feeling down.

Now it's time to dive in! Run the See Feel Hear Challenge just as you would anything else, by harmonizing the emotion that stems from the OCD conversation: *See* the emotion, *Feel* the emotion, and *Hear* the emotion with Infinite Love & Gratitude. When you get to the "hear" portion, listen to the voice of the emotion stemming from the OCD dialogue. Hear the beliefs that this voice is expressing about you. *Really, really listen.* This voice might say something really harsh, such as "You're a fucking idiot," "You're a worthless sack of shit," or "You'll never amount to anything." Whatever the voice says, respond with Infinite Love & Gratitude.

Now it's time to go into the black hole. What emotion does the voice cause you to feel? Shame? Sadness? Fear? Whatever the emotion is, run it through the SFH. *See* that emotion; *Feel* it. Once again, when you *Hear* the voice, *really listen*. What's the voice saying now about the beliefs you have about yourself?

It might be extremely negative, or it might not be. Regardless, whatever the voice says and whatever emotion it brings up for you, say, "Infinite Love & Gratitude."

Often when we're working with addictions, there's a spiraling loop into the depths of negativity, pessimism, and brokenness. Stay with this repeating process and ride this puppy down to the bottom. Remember, *riding a black hole to the bottom is a process that mirrors how the subconscious mind works.*

When you get to the light at the end of the tunnel and hear a positive voice, *really hear it.* Ask yourself what emotion you feel as you hear the positive voice. Especially when you're working with addictions, it's important to create a new pattern to replace the compulsive old pattern. For the sake of creating new neural pathways in your brain, do another SFH cycle based upon the positive emotion you're feeling from the new voice.

The Pink Elephant in the Room

There's one addiction that's particularly pleasurable that combines obsession and compulsion with a debilitating emotional addiction that operates at the lowest-frequency emotion on Dr. David R. Hawkins's consciousness scale: shame.[8] The ultimate unaddressed addiction in our modern world is undoubtedly porn, especially cyberporn and cybersex, where you can indulge any craving from straight sex to gay sex to sex with children, animals, and cadavers. You name it, and it's right there: sexual satiation and the satisfaction of your wildest fantasies, just a few clicks away in the privacy of your own home or office.

The instant availability and apparent invisibility and privacy of online sexual stimulation and interactive cybersex have created a booming addition to the regular porn industry and prostitution. By 2005 there were more than 420 million pornography pages available online.[9] According to comScore Media Metrix, 63.4 million Internet users viewed over 15 billion pages of adult content in one month alone. Annual Internet porn revenue figures are estimated to be anywhere up to $12 billion and growing.

Can anyone say "growing global addiction"?

The impact on families, relationships, pocketbooks, and the conscience of hooked individuals is incalculable. Although the average estimated online sex visit lasts only 14.6 minutes, the intensely pleasurable element of this particular addiction, plus ease of access, ensures that multiple hits are possible every day. The result? Ever-increasing obsessional patterns of sex-linked ideas, images, and thoughts that intrude into a person's thinking, making living a normal life difficult. Add in the secrecy and shame involved, and the price gets even higher.

An estimated 20 percent of all Internet porn involves children,[10] and kiddie porn is a $3 billion a year industry and one of the fastest growing online businesses.[11] This disturbing statistic alone shows how important greater awareness of this highly addictive "pastime" really is and how vitally society needs healing tools to effectively process addiction.

A Matter of Life and Death

Addiction is a potent mirror of humanity's general unrest and dissatisfaction. We've created a world of chronic *want.* We want more money, more phone apps, more burgers and buildings, more progress and technology, more time, more stock holdings, more security, and, yes, more sex. A restless species, we take pride in what we perceive as our spirited drive to accomplish and have things. Yet how fine is the line between *drive* and *driven!* And how seldom we peer behind the veil to see what's driving us.

Living from a deficit perspective, fixated on what we haven't got, we lack a sufficient inner wellspring of "feel good-ness" about ourselves to make the constant need for externally stimulating dopamine triggers unnecessary. It's hard to create a steady state of internal emotional satisfaction for no reason at all. But unless we want to forever chase after the sex glow, the success hit, and the

Ecstasy high to fill the emptiness inside, that's precisely what we need to do. And the See Feel Hear Challenge is a great tool to make this happen.

Addiction often marks the "make it or break it" point for people on their evolutionary paths. By driving themselves so far outside themselves in a desperate attempt to feel good, addiction becomes the ultimate crucible for transformation. And that's a harsh yet good thing. The dialogue is that of life or death: either the outside source of addiction wins, or the inner spirit of the being takes hold and the individual, catching a glimmer of the value of his or her own existence, at last chooses change.

❦

Part IV

CREATING CONSCIOUS CHANGE

Chapter 12

Getting from Here to There

"This moment this love comes to rest in me,
many beings in one being.
In one wheat grain a thousand sheaf stacks.
Inside the needle's eye, a turning night of stars."

— RUMI[1]

Congratulations! You've reached the point on this journey of love where you now know and can apply the See Feel Hear Challenge to even the most apparently difficult of life's circumstances. You have a sense of the science behind the Challenge and an understanding of the difficulties people might have in applying it to their lives. This last part of the book provides a brief summary—while going a little deeper into certain elements, such as manifestation, gratitude, and self-love—as well as additional suggestions for how to best apply the Challenge. Chapters 13 and 14 take a question-and-answer format, addressing questions you might have about the SFH Challenge process and more global issues for its application. Chapter 15 provides core-issue HUBs (heart's unprocessed beliefs) to use as maps to guide you into revealing and digesting the buried emotions and subconscious programs that most people hold around typical daily triggers.

A Broad-Spectrum Antidote

The reason why the See Feel Hear Challenge is so effective at helping people initiate constructive change and intentional creation is that it addresses two vital points concerning manifestation:

1. It shifts our perception about negativity. A lot of people think the trick to forging a happy future lies in getting rid of all the apparently negative thoughts and emotions they experience. But as we've seen, none of the symptoms and diseases we experience are actually negative; they're profound yet simple messages and opportunities for making the subconscious material that drives us. Realizing this shifts us from being

victims of circumstances to consciously evolving beings.

**2. It reveals emotion as the most effective door-
way to manifestation.** How we are present with emotion, feel it, observe it, discern it, intend it, imagine it,
and choose with it is the alchemical process of personal transformation. Emotion is the energy and oomph
of the creative process. Learning to be present with
our emotions—observing them, rather than reacting
to or avoiding them—we consciously harness their
power. Taking time to clearly see, feel, and hear our
emotional conversations gives us greater discernment
and insight into ourselves and others. Imagining our
intentions and feeling their emotional signature pro-
duces a powerful emotional attractor field that brings
us our heart's desires.

If we must "be it to have it"—and that's how manifestation indeed works—if we use the See Feel Hear Challenge to align our emotions and manifest our dreams, we
eventually realize that there's really nothing to get and
there's nowhere to go. If you already are what you desire
and you emanate its frequency, it's already part of you!
It's who you are, present in the now. What's to manifest?

Fighting addiction, insecurities, our spouses, the political system, and the "corporatocracy" just perpetuates

it all. If we want to make a change in the world, we have to realize that it's not about walking for cancer or fighting muscular dystrophy. The motto on the side of the Hall of Nations building at the United Nations in New York City proclaims: "Human beings are members of a whole, in creation of one essence and soul. If one member is afflicted with pain, other members uneasy will remain. If you have no sympathy for human pain, the name of human you cannot retain."

Global change occurs when we take individual responsibility for knowing what triggers us in the moment and, realizing that those things are simply our heart's unprocessed beliefs acting out, assimilating the buried wisdom and moving on. How much more powerful to see disease for what it is: a message, not a "thing" we're saddled with! How much more powerful to engage the *feeling* of health in present-time consciousness, imagining and emanating it rather than just thinking about it and wanting it—especially when we know that the emotion of want only confirms the lack of what we desire!

The Gratitude Action Potential

Valuing and appreciating your heart's calling for a new way of living is your *Gratitude Action Potential* (GAP). Embracing life with an attitude of gratitude is one of the keys to transforming pain into power, fear into courage, and stress into wisdom that you'd otherwise never know. Gratitude is love in action that bridges out of the darkness, revealing the "other side" and all the gaps and divisions in life. It heals separation, permitting easy access and communication, allowing two sides that would otherwise never come together to find common ground.

Bruce Lee was believed to have once stated, "Don't think; feel. It is like a finger pointing a way to the moon. Don't concentrate on the finger or else you'll miss all of the heavenly glory." So often there are circumstances in life that are painful, scary, and stressful, and the obvious value of the moment is not apparent. But these emotions are fingers pointing the way. Learning to say thank you for everything contained in life's journey acknowledges the Divine mastery and intelligence of the universe. Expressing gratitude acknowledges the truth that in an infinite universe, negative experiences aren't isolated. There are always positive aspects to balance them. It's just a matter of discovering them.

The attitude of gratitude evokes faith, love, and beauty where there was once only pain. It makes us aware that we are on a journey and that every step on the journey is equal in value. Instead of thinking that we need to get somewhere else, do something else, or be someone else in order to be whole, in gratitude we realize that everything is perfect now.

Bridging the GAP

Who is your adversary? The person who is on the so-called other side, from whom you feel so separate? The person who did something that you can never forgive or accept, let alone find value in his or her deed? What disease is in your body? What behavior do you constantly react with? Is there an addiction overpowering you? A way of thinking in which you feel you'll never be able to bridge the gap to another mind-set?

Take a moment to connect to this person, place, memory, disease, or addiction. What emotion does this trigger within you? Say, "Infinite Love & Gratitude." Know that you're part of an infinite universe. You're not alone. You're not the one person who is separate from All That Is. You're connected and part of everything. Hold the thought. Say, "Infinite Love & Gratitude." Know that you have free will to *respond* rather than react to any person, circumstance, or thought. Run the See Feel Hear Challenge.

> Practice this simple yet powerful shift in attitude. It only takes a brief moment. As you begin to respond rather than react to life, you'll start to notice new things. You'll witness your emotions beginning to shift as your heart opens and the painful feelings soften. This is the start of the journey toward self-love! This is bridging the GAP.

The Self-Love Garden

The most powerful healing force in the universe is self-love. It forms the foundation of the single, most important relationship in your life—with yourself. And don't you know that the strength of all your other relationships is exactly equal to the strength of this foundation? To love yourself is to be in awe of the miracle of your existence. It's to accept yourself as you are, with the "light" and "dark" parts, all the while knowing that the real you lies beyond all perceived matter-based dualities. Self-love is knowing your values and boundaries, and honoring them authentically; it's about teaching others how to treat you by showing them how you treat yourself; it's about being kind and compassionate toward the person who's looking back at you in the mirror; and it's about looking after your mind, your body, and your spirit, knowing that you are worth the care.

A Wonderful Practice for Developing Self-Love

Ask yourself, "What do I most need to hear from others?" Is it that they love you, admire you, accept you as you are, appreciate you, forgive you? Write down whatever comes up for you. Do your best to exhaust your list of needs!

You'll find that what you most want to hear from others is what you most need to tell yourself.

Run the See Feel Hear Challenge on this list. Look in the mirror and say these things to yourself twice a day, morning and night. Include them in your meditation or creative visualization sessions. Know that you are creating a powerful positive attractor field for your life, and that soon you will enjoy a greater sense of self-love and inner peace than you ever had before.

Benevolent Gardening

Your life is your garden, and you must plant the seeds of your ideas, dreams, and choices, nurturing them to get the best harvest—meaning the greatest you—possible.

So exactly how do you nurture the garden of your life? Here's a six-step process that will empower you to create a flourishing life:

1. Gratitude

2. Assess/Action

3. Research

4. Diligence

5. Empty

6. Nature/Nurture

1. Gratitude

Gardening starts when you recognize that you have a need or desire. Whether it's to save money or eat more healthily, this desire is your compass throughout the creation process. Feeling gratitude for your life and your heart's desires empowers them! Be grateful for that healthy body or that new job you want, because being grateful means you've already aligned yourself with the reality of them and claimed them as yours.

2. Assess/Action

When you make the decision to change your life, it's important to assess what type lifestyle you'd like to have. Do you want economic freedom? Travel? More time with family and friends? Deeper spiritual connection? All of the above? Once your choices are made, make a list of things you desire. Be sure to include The Five Basics for Optimal Health: *water, food, rest, exercise,* and *owning your power.* The quantity, quality, and frequency of The Five Basics are essential acts of self-love that will turbocharge your health, wealth, and relationships. (To learn more about The 5 Basics in detail, you can find them in Darren's book *The Power of Infinite Love & Gratitude.*)

3. Research

Once you know what you want, research the most appealing avenues for achieving that vision. If you want healthier finances, will something as simple as opening a savings account work for you? Or maybe you want to start a business? Think about all the ways in which you can transform your current situation, starting from where you are *right now.*

4. Diligence

Keep your word to yourself! If you say you're going to exercise, then exercise. If you say you're going to drink two quarts of pure water a day, then drink your water. Keep a protective eye on the garden of your life. When negative thoughts and overwhelming feelings that can destroy your hard work get activated, realize that a subconscious, reactive pattern is in motion, and use the See Feel Hear Challenge to process and own it!

5. Empty

Empty your mind and open your heart to receive your harvest. When you do the previous four steps, emptying naturally occurs. Observe the quietness within your mind and heart. Allow rather than resist the natural process of blooming that stems from being in alignment with your goals. Remember, a garden doesn't need to be forced to bear fruit. In this nonreactive, "empty" space, your life will flower.

6. Nature/Nurture

The essence of who you are is a continually thriving, growing, changing being. Follow the simple steps of the See Feel Hear Challenge and begin to build your garden in a doable, strategic way. Before you know it, you'll be experiencing the life you once only dreamed of.

Creating a Life Vision

A life vision is a powerful launching pad, a viewpoint from which to create powerful goals and inspiring action plans. It's transformational and energizing, and it uplifts your state of being into the higher realms of possibility, joy, and creativity.

What truly inspires you? What does the big picture of your greatest possibilities for your life look like? Once you get in touch with your life's vision, it becomes the inspiration for your every idea and action, because *it isn't a landing place or a destination.* Vision isn't a "future" reality; it's already part of you, and you can see, feel, and hear it right now.

Steps for Accessing Your Life Vision

First quiet your mind by entering into a state of meditation that takes you out of day-to-day concerns into the space of presence and peace, where you can hear the inner voice of your higher self.

Imagine the highest possibility for your life, letting your creativity expand until it touches the passionate spark that lives in the center of your heart. Here is where you'll discover your soul's calling. Trust and surrender to receiving your soul's messages, regardless of how outrageous they may be. This is the Divine speaking to you.

Run a See Feel Hear Challenge on the soulful connection you're making with your vision. What emotion do you experience? Whether it's a so-called positive or negative emotion, allow yourself to digest and process the emotion evoked by your vision. See the images, thoughts, and pictures that are forming in your mind. Place your hand in the "I love you" gesture and acknowledge each one, saying, "Infinite Love & Gratitude." Feel in your heart and body what it's like to make this Divine connection. "Infinite Love & Gratitude."

Listen to the voice inside of your mind. Hear what it's saying to you about your beliefs around your life vision. "Infinite Love & Gratitude." If the voice was anything other than positive, empowering, or confident, stay with the voice and bring out the next emotion that's triggered by the negative voice. Go through this again and again until you discover the comforting light of your highest truth. Trust the process and let it take you wherever it wants to go. It will absolutely eventually bring you to a transformed space.

As best you can, write down everything you experienced during this See Feel Hear Challenge. Describe how it feels to be living in alignment with your life vision from the core of your being.

❧

Chapter 13

Questions about the
See Feel Hear Challenge

*"The body itself is a screen to shield and partially
reveal the light that's blazing inside your presence."*

— R u m i [1]

In the following two chapters, we take a more conversational approach to the See Feel Hear Challenge. As a newcomer to the See Feel Hear Challenge, Cate asks Darren some of the questions about the process that came up for her while she was learning it. Darren also delves deep into some very thorny metaphysical questions about personal choice and the subconscious.

Cate: *The more I do the See Feel Hear Challenge, the easier and faster it becomes. However, like most people, I've got a lot on my plate, and I've realized that one of the easiest excuses for not doing the See Feel Hear Challenge is, "I don't have time." As if I don't have a few minutes a day to change my life for the better! But in general, how long should the process take?*

Darren: Ah Cate, that old "should" question. All in all, there's no cookie-cutter approach. How long the process takes depends upon the moment you're in. In less than 15 seconds, you could have an immediate shift. Or, depending on how deeply you want to get into it, it could take half an hour or more. On average I'd say it takes around five to ten minutes. Once you get good at it and understand the process, within 60 seconds there can be a powerful shift in perception.

Cate: *I've found that often just acknowledging what I'm feeling and tuning in to it is enough to make a big difference.*

Darren: Exactly! Just observing the emotions, knowing that we wouldn't choose whatever perceived negative emotion we're feeling toward symptoms or stressors, begins the shift. Observing is the first step toward taking responsibility for consciously manifesting. The body is intelligently designed to heal, regenerate, and be whole, and processing and digesting emotions empowers the system to create balance and to sustainably change.

There are many factors to creating a healthy body, mind, and life. Plenty of people who are eating the right foods, drinking the right amount of water, exercising daily, and taking supplements like an addict are still suffering. My intention in sharing the See Feel Hear Challenge is to empower individuals from the inside out, to move through any and all life experiences.

Cate: *Sometimes I get triggered, and then observing seems out of the question. For example, I'll be talking to my ex, and bam, stuff comes up. What can I do in situations where I'm in a heated conversation?*

Darren: If something happens or somebody says something that triggers a negative feeling, I encourage you to immediately run a See Feel Hear Challenge in the moment.

Cate: *How can I possibly do that in the middle of an argument?*

Darren: It's difficult at first, because when we're in it, we're in it; when the subconscious mind has been triggered, we're hijacked. And it takes a real, conscious effort to put ourselves back in the observer role. However, it's an investment that will really pay off over time. It's a healthy thing to be able to step away for a minute and say, "You know what? I've got to take a moment. No disrespect intended. I'll be right back." And you walk away.

After you've done a quick See Feel Hear Challenge, you'll have a different view toward the situation that will have a direct impact in shifting the conflict.

Another approach is to stay right with the person, but connect to your observer self through asking the truth question. Politely request, "Hold on a second," and close your eyes and take a deep breath. Acknowledge your feelings; say (or think), "Infinite Love & Gratitude to this"; and ask yourself the truth question: "Would I consciously choose to feel this way right now? Would I choose to be in a conflict? Hell no! What am I choosing to feel right now? I am choosing to feel compassion. I am compassion. I am compassion. I am compassion. How does it feel to imagine this? Grateful." Boom! You've shifted the whole tone of the argument in under 15 seconds by discerning where you are, setting an intention, and creating a new feeling tone through your imagination—all in the privacy of your own mind.

Cate: *And when I shift, automatically the other person has space to shift.*

Darren: Right. We're all interconnected. When I can move myself from judgment and anger to a heart space of discernment, love is immediately infused into the perceived conflict.

Cate: *When I'm doing the process, sometimes I find that I don't see anything or hear any words. And sometimes I can't seem to feel any real emotion. What can people do when that happens?*

Darren: Observe that you don't see anything. Observe that. See nothing. "Infinite Love & Gratitude." Observe that you're not feeling anything. "Infinite Love & Gratitude." Recognize that you don't hear anything. "Infinite Love & Gratitude." That's your subconscious mind speaking, too! The subconscious will only release what you are consciously able to process in the moment, based upon the consciousness of the intention you set.

Cate: *What do you mean by that?*

Darren: I find that most people, when setting an intention, do so out of fear rather than love. They're focused on getting away from something or preventing something from happening, rather than genuinely focusing on where their hearts are leading them. Love always moves toward things; fear always moves away. A fear-based intention will keep a person anchored to the current situation he or she is in.

Cate: *How do I know whether or not I'm creating a heart-based intention?*

Darren: Listen. The most important thing you can do is just listen. As Commissioner Gordon has a direct line to Batman, your heart has a direct line to the Universe. Close your eyes, take a deep breath, put your hand over your heart center in the "I love you" gesture, and listen. The Universe speaks to all of us through our hearts. If you stay with it long enough, something will come.

Cate: *What if I hear or see something that's horrific? What if the voice from the Universe says something abusive and destructive?*

Darren: When the subconscious shows up as a voice that's expressing itself in a frightful way, such as a feeling of brokenness, a scary vision, a disease pattern, or pain in the body, I immediately ask the truth question. It always puts everything in the proper perspective, which reminds me that I would never consciously choose any of those things.

For the most part, the role of our subconscious mind is completely misunderstood. Horrific as some of the messages from our subconscious might be, they aren't meant to scare or hurt us. They're meant to show us something about ourselves: information we need to see, feel, and hear in order to recognize our personal truth. With that understanding, we discover that whatever the subconscious dishes up is really okay.

Cate: *But some of the things that show up from the sub-conscious really aren't okay, like brain tumors in little children and murder and rape.*

Darren: You've got a great point. However, there's a human point of view and a consciousness point of view: human law versus universal law. In the human world, those things aren't okay. From the universal perspective of "we're all one," all life circumstances have a bigger meaning and purpose than our conscious minds can perceive and process. How can it be perceived as okay that children are starving or homeless or being sexually abused? How can it be okay that people are losing their homes and nest eggs? Is it okay? It is what it is. Do these horrific things create real feelings that at times are excruciating? Of course, and that's okay, too.

Making sense out of things that don't appear to make any sense whatsoever is hugely challenging. There's a component of faith that's interwoven into the equation. You have to trust that what comes up needs to come up.

Cate: *It's pretty tough to accept thoughts that tell us to hurt ourselves or other people, or thoughts of rage about the world and what's going on.*

Darren: Would you really choose to hurt yourself or others? Hell no! And yet, to some degree or another, we all have internal dialogue that's destructive, setting hurtful external actions into motion. The point is, when we recognize that it's not "us" choosing these things, but rather the subconscious at the helm of this ship running autopilot programs based upon beliefs and emotional patterns that aren't even ours, then all the perceived wacko things that happen in our minds and on this planet suddenly begin to make sense. Somehow, all these things, no matter how heinous, are a means to protect a part of ourselves so that we can grow in the present moment. They're a feedback mechanism.

Given the choice, would anyone ever choose these things? Do people choose tragedy? Hell no! That's why it's tragedy.

Cate: *So you're saying that the guys who got into planes and flew them into the World Trade Center really didn't choose to do what they did?*

Darren: Wow. What a delicate, brutally triggering question! To the family and friends of the people who died on 9/11, Infinite Love & Gratitude. To the people whose children were massacred in Sandy Hook, Connecticut, Infinite Love & Gratitude. To the people killed and maimed at the Boston Marathon, Infinite Love & Gratitude. This is the ultimate question: At what point do we choose love in the face of anger, outrage, and fear? At what point does the buck stop? When do we cease contributing to the ripples of destruction and recognize that we are all a responsible part of the whole?

There were choices made in each and every one of these horrific and inexcusable experiences. However, the choices that were made were made by individuals perceiving life through a reactive lens. In no way does this justify their actions. But understanding this does help us to stop reacting to *their* violent reactions by appreciating the role that the subconscious mind is playing in these kinds of events. All reactions are subconscious in nature, and there is no judgment or choice when the reactive mind is triggered. Simply put, the reactive mind reacts, and once a subconscious program or emotional pattern is set into motion, it stays that way until met by another force. Fear will not transform fear, hate will not transform hate, judgment will not transform violence. Only love has the power to create sustainable change.

At what point do we see it all as a form of dialogue rather than victimization? This is really, really tough if you're talking about my baby dying or my husband, son, or sister being blown apart. The immediate reaction is to lash out and kill in return. And on and on it goes. Where it stops, no one knows.

For healing and growth to occur, regardless of everything that's gone on, it's important that we bypass our conscious perceptions and judgments about the many tragedies of our modern-day world and start processing the subconscious causes so that we can choose love in the face of fear, thereby securing a peaceful world for all our children.

To know one thing is to know a thousand different things. When we can appreciate that a headache or anxiety is a feedback mechanism for an individual person to wake up in the moment, we can also extrapolate to the big picture of the world. The tragedy of 9/11, the Holocaust, the Rwandan Genocide, the Trail of Tears—all are collective conscious symptoms to awaken us to a deeper truth: that we're being driven by collective subconscious beliefs and protective patterns that originate from our ancestors thousands of years ago. But here's the flip side to it: the powerful impact of 9/11 was that so many people around the world ended up funneling their consciousness into this horror with their hearts focusing on compassion, love, and the safest outcomes for the people involved. And that's a beautiful thing.

Who isn't sad and horrified on some level by each of the situations I just mentioned. But I know, deep in my heart, that we would never choose to feel sad and that we would never choose to feel horrified. The fact that we're feeling this way lets us know that these emotions are also a by-product of limiting beliefs that ultimately are subconscious programs as well.

So now I can answer your question. The world we live in today is fully reactive. It's a fight, fright, and flight atmosphere, and we're ping-ponging from one reactive component of life to the next in every arena, from economics to the environment, health care to politics. All are facets of a reactive world that has no understanding of itself and the role that the subconscious mind is playing in the individual and collective experience. And the consequence of this lack of understanding is that pain, fear, and stress have escalated into a state of global suffering. From my perspective, the only recourse is to create authentic dialogue by getting to the root of the subconscious emotional patterns that are driving those reactive behaviors. From there we can begin to foster understanding and create a safe space to heal.

Cate: *When our programs are running the show, where do we begin?*
Darren: Infinite Love & Gratitude.

Cate: *That's too simple.*
Darren: With all the chaos and suffering in the world, we believe that solutions have to be complicated. But needing to make things difficult is just another core belief. The truth is, anything that's complicated isn't the truth. The truth is as simple as listening to your heart and as complicated as the answer it gives you.

Cate: *Sometimes it's hard to tune in to the words and feel Infinite Love & Gratitude. I mean, I can feel love and gratitude. But <u>infinite</u> is a pretty tall order! Is just thinking or saying it enough?*

Darren: I have a friend who used to joke with me about that. "Does it have to be infinite? Can't it just be 'a lot of love and gratitude'?" Developing a relationship with Infinite Love & Gratitude is an important step in your evolution and that of humanity. Feeling the consciousness of Infinite Love & Gratitude will bring you to a whole other level. But just saying or thinking it is enough. Be patient with yourself. Feelings, for the most part on planet Earth, are something we're evolving into. Feeling is the heart of the matter. If we were already in touch with our feelings, we'd be so much nicer to ourselves and those around us.

Chapter 14

Questions about the See Feel Hear Challenge and the Mind and Body

"Water, stories, the body, all the things we do, are mediums that hide and show what's hidden."

— RUMI[1]

Cate: *Over the last few years, I've had two dear friends die of cancer, and another close friend currently has stage 4 brain cancer. How can people who are facing such extreme health challenges use the See Feel Hear Challenge?*

Darren: Those are tough situations. First I'd have the person connect to the experience and start with the truth question: "Would I choose this? Hell no!" No one ever chooses any disease, let alone cancer. Then the next thing to do is set an intention. Everything is energy, including this disease, and the purpose of the See Feel Hear Challenge is to process whatever emotions are tied into it. Cancer is a big HUB.

Cate: *What do you mean by that?*

Darren: There's more to cancer than just cancer. It represents the heart's unprocessed beliefs (HUB). It's a symptom that has an enormous amount of attached energy in the form of meaning, emotions, and situations. Cancer forms the HUB for other triggering circumstances that are related to it. For example, it's difficult to think of the word *cancer* without other associated triggers such as chemotherapy, radiation, and bald women, showing up. So, Cate, connect to the word *cancer,* and think about it for a moment. What comes up for you?

Cate: *Fear. That's the first thing. I can feel it. It's visceral.*

Darren: Perfect. Fear is your starting gate. It's your portal of possibilities. Current research says that one out of every two men and one out of every two women will develop cancer in their lifetimes.[2]

Obviously this is a deep dialogue. Everyone who is asked to connect to the word *cancer* will have some type of emotional charge come up. There's no one today who's not personally affected by it. Remember, Cate, we're looking for anything that triggers pain, fear, and stress, because they're the gateway to the subconscious mind. Cancer is an obvious portal. When people mention cancer, they whisper or call it the *C* word. The cancer HUB has that much power over them.

Cate: *No kidding. When I ask my friend if she wants to learn the See Feel Hear Challenge to get to the subconscious emotions driving the cancer, she just changes the subject. And she rarely utters the word <u>cancer</u>. So what can you do for people like that?*

Darren: There's nothing to do. No one needs to be fixed. We're already whole. That behavior is a protective pattern. What you can do is observe how you react emotionally to them and run the See Feel Hear Challenge with yourself so that you can shift your perception about the circumstances. Stay in your heart. Remember, when you're observing someone who's in a subconscious reactive state, you're not really seeing her for who she is in the moment. You're actually catching a glimpse of her as a little girl in a protective state that reveals itself as a gift in strange wrapping paper.

Cate: *How about the person who does want to dive in and engage cancer in a dialogue? In the thick of the experience, everything is so emotionally charged. What do you suggest?*

Darren: With something like cancer or being abused, there are so many emotional triggers. Just go after it. Go through the black holes. Remember that at the point of complete darkness is the beginning of light. Dive in! Process the emotions as many times a day as things come up. What could be more important than seeing, feeling, and hearing the hidden emotions in the subconscious that are driving cancer or abuse? Just know that when you stay with it, you'll come through transformed.

Cate: *At my friend's house, everything is about her cancer. The whole conversation, 24/7, is about the food she can or can't eat, her pills, her schedules, her therapies, her weight, what the next move should or shouldn't be. There's no escape from it. How can you possibly process all that?*

Darren: Infinite Love & Gratitude. The most insidious thing that happens is that we become enmeshed in the cancer conversation or the ADD conversation or the addiction conversation, and all the attached programs to these things catch us like a spiderweb. We wear pink ribbons and buttons saying, "I'm a survivor." We read all the books. An entire identity forms around cancer, like the spokes of a wheel around a HUB.

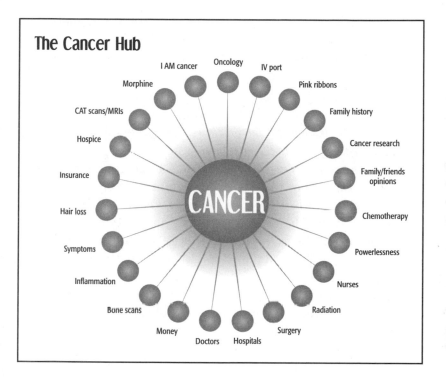

The Cancer Hub

I AM cancer
Oncology
IV port
Morphine
Pink ribbons
CAT scans/MRIs
Family history
Hospice
Cancer research
Insurance
Family/friends opinions
CANCER
Hair loss
Chemotherapy
Symptoms
Powerlessness
Inflammation
Nurses
Bone scans
Radiation
Money
Surgery
Doctors
Hospitals

Rather than focusing on what we want, which is health, we end up consumed by the experience. And the experience and the cancer grow.

It's really difficult to talk about this in a way that's heartfelt. But here's the thing: We're actually not even talking about cancer. We're acknowledging that our hearts have unprocessed beliefs. Cancer is just an extremely emotionally charged doorway. Remember that e-motion is the foundation of creation, and emotions are what move us. They're literally doorways to parts of ourselves that are unknown, taking us into uncharted territory.

Cate: *It's a pretty tall order to ask people to see cancer as an exciting ride into the unknown.*

Darren: It's a really hard truth to accept. Tell the four-year-old boy who just lost his mommy to breast cancer that she missed a great doorway. Or say that to the woman whose best friend of 40 years just died from lung cancer. Tell these people that cancer is a gift in strange wrapping paper, and they'll spit in your eye. Our human identity goes into such despair and sorrow. It shouts, "I hate cancer. I want to destroy it!" But the heart of the matter is, even though it's natural and easy to be angry, regretful, depressed, and fearful about it, the emotional conversation of cancer holds tremendous vistas of possibilities if we'll just engage in that conversation.

Cate: *You often say that we don't actually heal anything. So where does the real medicine of the See Feel Hear Challenge lie?*

Darren: Feeling is the medicine. As soon as you can feel the emotion surrounding a new intention, as soon as you can hear its voice, as soon as you see through its eyes, you're triggering a whole new pharmacy. The body and brain simply follow what you put in front of them.

Cate: *This is why the placebo effect works so well.*

Darren: It's incredible! We say, "Here, this pill is going to help you." And even though it's just a sugar pill, it helps people. Traditional research indicates that placebos work about 30 percent of the time. But many scientific studies indicate that the figure might be a lot higher. Dr. Herbert Benson, founder of the Benson-Henry Institute for Mind Body Medical in Boston and a professor at Harvard Medical School, says it might work up to 90 percent of the time.[3] There's also something called the *nocebo effect*.

Cate: *The nocebo effect?*

Darren: The exact opposite of the placebo effect. It's where a person is told he has four weeks to live, and boom!—he lives right up to the term of the prognosis. Have you ever seen the film *The Matrix*?

Cate: *Sure.*

Darren: Remember the part where Neo walks in and the child is bending spoons with his mind? He gives the child an inquisitive look, like, "How're you doing that?" And the child responds that one must realize that essentially there is no spoon—that the spoon and everything else in his "reality" are the products of his own mind.

The same is true when it comes to healing. How do you heal cancer? There is no cancer. There's simply a subconscious conversation going on with your body that you're not aware of until the symptoms show up.

Cate: *And ultimately the most healing power of all lies in the heart—in finally being able to feel love for one's own being.*

Darren: Get this. The thymus gland is ultimately the powerhouse of our immunity. It's enormous when we're born, and guess what it's in direct alignment with? The heart chakra. The heart is also the bridge between the three lower chakras and the three above: it's the bridge between the physical and the spiritual. It's the bridge of love.

When there's a limiting-belief program in the heart chakra, people are more prone to suffering with immune challenges, because they have programs that limit them from loving themselves. There's a disconnect between who they really are—loving, spiritual beings—and who they subconsciously believe themselves to be. So the ultimate question to ask for boosting your immune system in any given moment is, "Who am I?" because the immune system is all about telling self from nonself.

Cate: *Wow! Look at the connection with cancer! It's a disease that has no boundaries, because the immune system can't tell healthy cells from cancer cells anymore.*

Darren: Bingo! The trouble is, "Who am I?" is also about the last question most of us have an answer for. I have to be this person because mom is really insecure and afraid, and that person because Dad is angry, volatile, and unpredictable. I have to be totally another way for my friends to like me. We learn how to be different people in different circumstances. This is not from conscious choice. It's protection. It's a program.

Cate: *So while I'm playing the sexpot to keep my man satisfied, and juggling the Pollyanna act with my parents and the Queen of Deadlines role for my editors, I'm killing myself by being things that aren't in alignment with my heart?*

Darren: If any of those things is an act, then yes. More than anything, be real. Be honest with yourself. Love yourself. Start asking, "Who am I in my marriage?" "Who am I as a parent?" "Who am I as a son or daughter?" "Who am I as a human being?" "Who am I as a child of God?" "Who am I?" And when you start asking these different questions, pay attention to the emotional charges that start going off inside.

Cate: *What about conventional treatments for disease? How can the See Feel Hear Challenge work in alignment with them?*

Darren: Whatever treatment plan you choose, every step along the way, keep doing the See Feel Hear Challenge. Dialogue with the hepatitis or the asthma throughout the day. When you walk into the doctor's office or the hospital, ask yourself, "What emotion am I feeling here? When I'm talking to this doctor, what am I feeling?" When you're at the office and somebody asks, "How are you doing?" what emotions come up? When you go home and talk to your husband or wife, your mother or brother, what emotions are you feeling? Always start at the HUB with whatever disease is getting your attention. Then start to look at all the spokes of the wheel, the people and situations that are constantly feeding the situation and keeping it in motion.

Cate: *What if you're in a lot of pain, and it's really hard to focus on setting intentions and doing the See Feel Hear Challenge? What can you do?*

Darren: If you're talking bone-cancer pain, war-shrapnel pain, fibromyalgia pain; if you're talking acute emotional pain from abuse, rape, or an accident and you're maxed out, you can keep it simple by just using the hand gesture and saying, "Infinite Love & Gratitude" over and over. The brain has a difficult time focusing on two things at once. So shifting your focus from the pain to Infinite Love & Gratitude helps so much. But I want to emphasize something: chronic pain, whatever form it takes, is emotional. Go into it. Dig into the emotion. What are you unwilling to let go of? What are you unable to forgive? Ask yourself these questions. Whatever comes up, run a See Feel Hear Challenge. Infinite Love & Gratitude.

Cate: *In the process of intentional living, sometimes relationships simply don't work out. Is it possible to create a peaceful disconnect from a person or a situation?*

Darren: It all comes down to honest dialogue, starting with yourself. Be true to your heart and express yourself in a loving way. Honor people wherever they're at, and honor the parts of yourself that have a hard time with any of these things. Process the emotions within yourself so that you can move in the direction that's true to your heart, because that's always the right direction to be moving in. Your choices might not make sense to other people, including the person you're looking to disconnect with. But if you're coming from the heart, chances are it's not really a disconnection showing up, just a reconnection in a different way; you're just reestablishing your boundaries in a healthy way. Life is change, and all relationships, no matter what kind they are, are going to evolve.

Cate: *Society places so much emphasis on consistency in earning, in relationships, in career. We're expected to stick* *with one thing and one person our whole lives. But is that even realistic?*

Darren: Our expectations about so many things in the world are based upon what we've been told, not necessarily what they're really about. People get married, have kids, and do their thing, and half the time they get divorced. Imagine how wonderful it would be for struggling couples to have the See Feel Hear Challenge to consciously process the dramas and traumas of an ever-evolving relationship!

The importance of developing authentic dialogue and journeying into the heart of the matter applies full spectrum: from the individual to the couple, the couple to the family, the family to the community, the community to the world, and then the world back to the individual. Our ability to bridge perceived gaps and differences into meaningful and purposeful experiences is not just fundamental for reframing disease, divorce, trauma, drama, and war. It also liberates human beings in a way that our planet has yet to experience.

Cate: *So where do we go from here?*

Darren: I invite you into the heart of the matter, my friend. In your heart, you'll discover a menu of infinite possibilities. Embrace them with your inner child's passion for life and imagination and, most of all, with Infinite Love & Gratitude. Keep shining bright!

Chapter 15

The Heart's Unprocessed Beliefs—The HUB for Discovering Gifts in Strange Wrapping Paper

"Let yourself be silently drawn by the strange pull of what you really love. It will not lead you astray."

— RUMI[1]

We think they come out of nowhere: migraines, indigestion, quarrels with loved ones, cancer, sprained ankles. But there's an invisible cause involved. Just as the unseen force of gravity drops apples on our heads, so subconscious, undigested emotions drop wake-up calls into our lives. Once we see them for what they are—our heart's unprocessed beliefs—with the proper tools, we can effectively use these fabulous messengers as the opportunities they are to change our lives forever for the better.

The HUBs in the following diagrams represent a few typical messengers that show up in our lives. Every spoke on each wheel is a potential emotional trigger related to that particular symptom, stressor, or intention. Which ones trigger an emotional charge in you? Follow up on them! Use the See Feel Hear Challenge and process them! This is how you dig down into your subconscious to unearth the gold lying within.

Use these HUBs as guides to map the emotional charges that lurk at the heart of the symptoms and stressors you're experiencing and the intentions you're now creating. If you notice, each spoke on every HUB can be a HUB in its own right, with ever-more-subtle spokes or triggers emanating from them. On a few of the HUBs, such as the relationship, health, and happiness HUBs, both "positive" and "negative" situations are listed, since both can serve as triggers! And if all of this looks a little overwhelming, remember: each HUB and every spoke is a path to love—of self, of others, and of the world.

Infinite Love & Gratitude!

Five Physical-Symptom HUBs

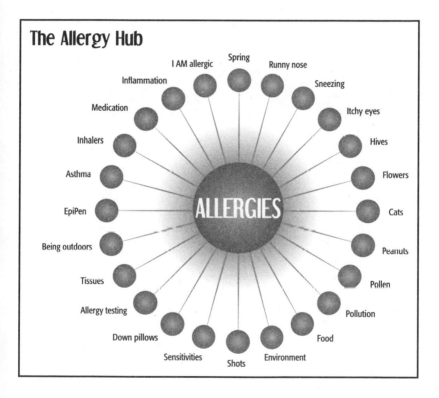

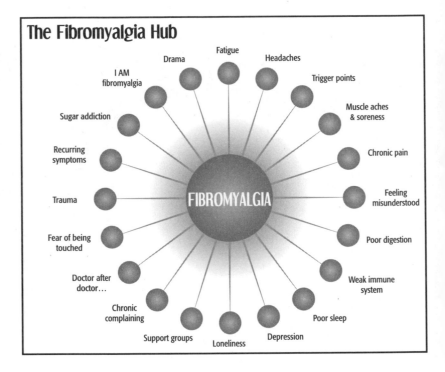

The Fibromyalgia Hub

FIBROMYALGIA

- Fatigue
- Drama
- I AM fibromyalgia
- Sugar addiction
- Recurring symptoms
- Trauma
- Fear of being touched
- Doctor after doctor…
- Chronic complaining
- Support groups
- Loneliness
- Depression
- Poor sleep
- Weak immune system
- Poor digestion
- Feeling misunderstood
- Chronic pain
- Muscle aches & soreness
- Trigger points
- Headaches

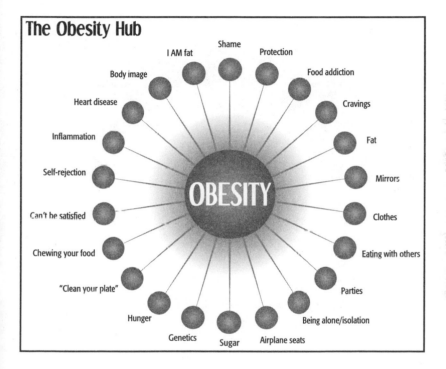

The Obesity Hub

Shame
I AM fat
Protection
Body image
Food addiction
Heart disease
Cravings
Inflammation
Fat
Self-rejection
Mirrors

OBESITY

Can't be satisfied
Clothes
Chewing your food
Eating with others
"Clean your plate"
Parties
Hunger
Being alone/isolation
Genetics
Sugar
Airplane seats

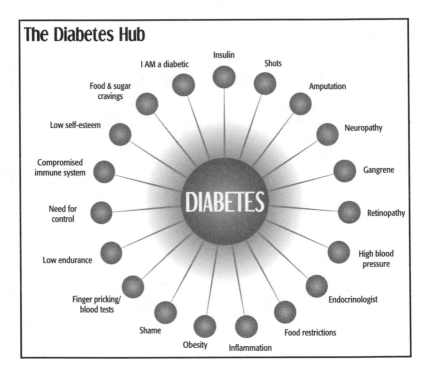

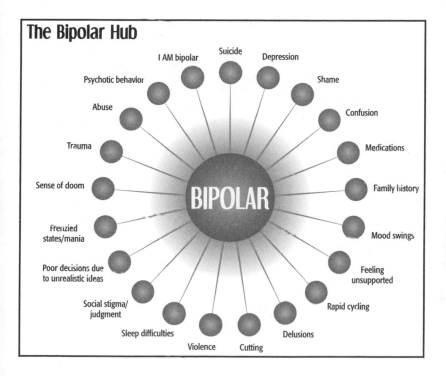

The Bipolar Hub

I AM bipolar · Suicide · Depression · Shame · Psychotic behavior · Confusion · Abuse · Medications · Trauma · Family history · Sense of doom · BIPOLAR · Mood swings · Frenzied states/mania · Feeling unsupported · Poor decisions due to unrealistic ideas · Rapid cycling · Social stigma/judgment · Delusions · Sleep difficulties · Cutting · Violence

Five Stressor HUBs

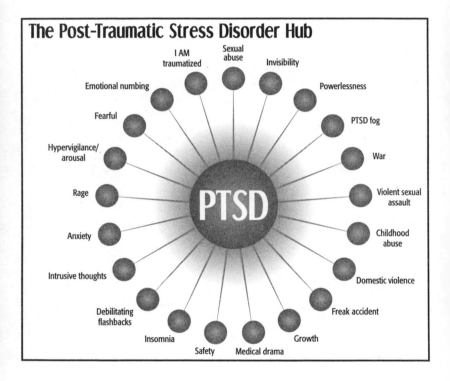

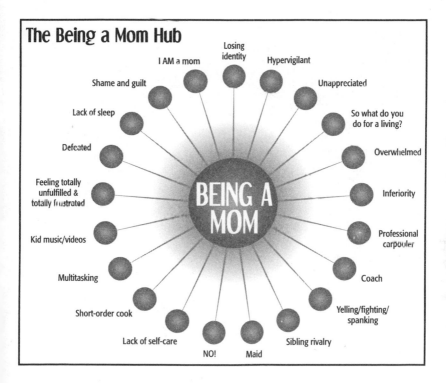

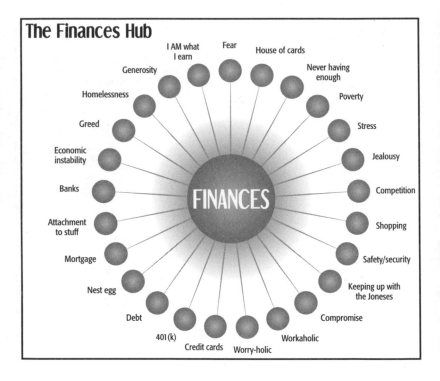

The Finances Hub

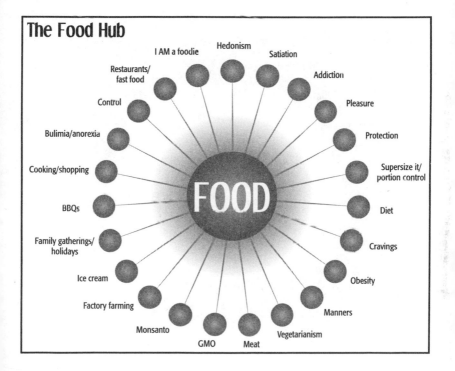

The Food Hub

I AM a foodie · Hedonism · Satiation · Addiction · Pleasure · Protection · Supersize it/portion control · Diet · Cravings · Obesity · Manners · Vegetarianism · Meat · GMO · Monsanto · Factory farming · Ice cream · Family gatherings/holidays · BBQs · Cooking/shopping · Bulimia/anorexia · Control · Restaurants/fast food

FOOD

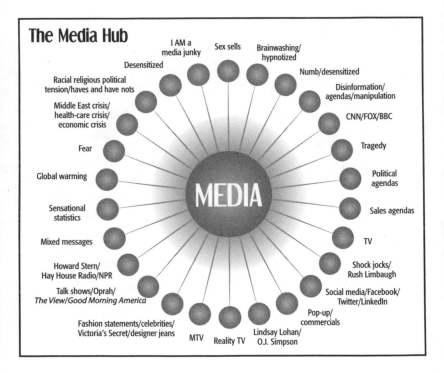

The Media Hub

I AM a media junky · Sex sells · Brainwashing/hypnotized · Desensitized · Numb/desensitized · Racial religious political tension/haves and have nots · Disinformation/agendas/manipulation · Middle East crisis/health-care crisis/economic crisis · CNN/FOX/BBC · Fear · Tragedy · Global warming · Political agendas · Sensational statistics · Sales agendas · Mixed messages · TV · Howard Stern/Hay House Radio/NPR · Shock jocks/Rush Limbaugh · Talk shows/Oprah/The View/Good Morning America · Social media/Facebook/Twitter/LinkedIn · Fashion statements/celebrities/Victoria's Secret/designer jeans · Pop-up/commercials · MTV · Reality TV · Lindsay Lohan/O.J. Simpson

MEDIA

Five Intention HUBs

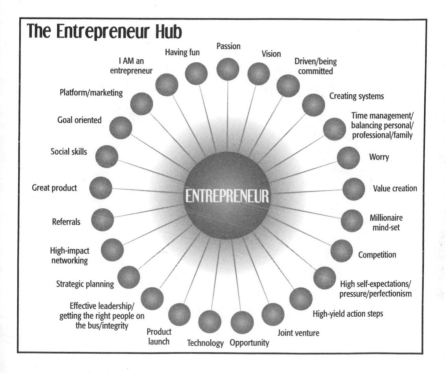

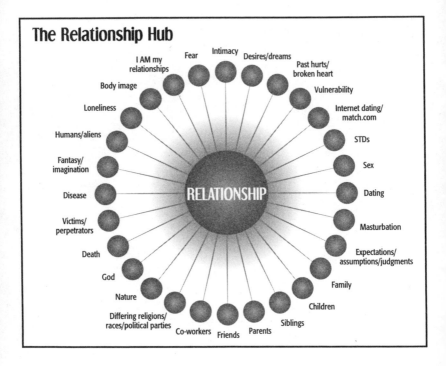

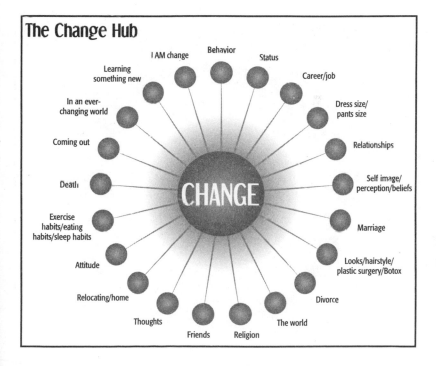

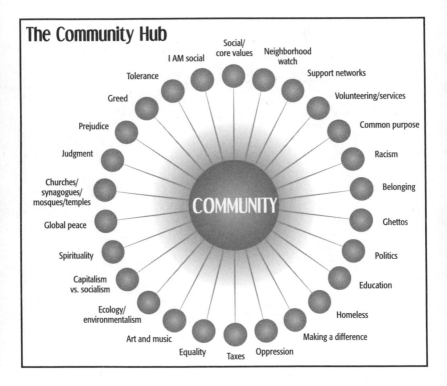

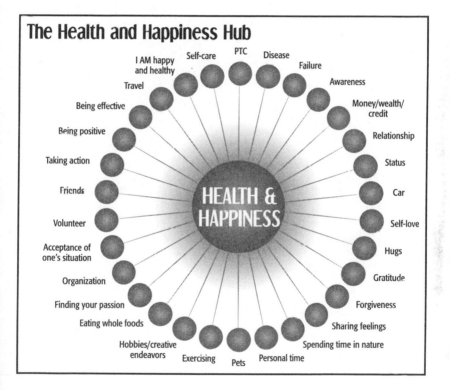

The Health and Happiness Hub

HEALTH & HAPPINESS

I AM happy and healthy · Self-care · PTC · Disease · Failure · Awareness · Money/wealth/credit · Relationship · Status · Car · Self-love · Hugs · Gratitude · Forgiveness · Sharing feelings · Spending time in nature · Personal time · Pets · Exercising · Hobbies/creative endeavors · Eating whole foods · Finding your passion · Organization · Acceptance of one's situation · Volunteer · Friends · Taking action · Being positive · Being effective · Travel

ENDNOTES

Preface by Dr. Darren Weissman

1. See Lori M. Hilt, Christine B. Cha, and Susan Nolen-Hoeksema's paper "Nonsuicidal Self-injury in Young Adolescent Girls: Moderators of the Distress-Function Relationship," in *Journal of Consulting and Clinical Psychology*, vol. 76 (1): pp 63–71 (2008).

2. See Centers for Disease Control and Prevention, *Public Health Action Plan to Integrate Mental Health Promotion and Mental Illness Prevention with Chronic Disease Prevention*, 2011–2015 (Atlanta, GA: U.S. Department of Health and Human Services, 2011).

3. See L. A. Pratt, D. J. Brody, and Q. Gu's paper "Antidepressant Use in Persons Aged 12 and Over: United States, 2005–2008," http://www.cdc.gov/nchs/data/databriefs/db76.pdf. NCHS data brief, no 76 (Hyattsville, MD: National Center for Health Statistics, 2011).

4. See Centers for Disease Control and Prevention, "Chronic Diseases and Health Promotion: Chronic Diseases Are the Leading Causes of Death and Disability in the U.S.," http://www.cdc.gov/chronicdisease/overview/index.htm (2012).

5. See Angela Zimm's article "Children Sicker Now Than in Past, Harvard Report Says": http://www.bloomberg.com/apps/new s?pid=newsarchive&sid=a8jD2znv51pU.

6. See Divorce Statistics: http://www.divorcestatistics.info/ divorce-statistics-and-divorce-rate-in-the-usa.html.

7. See Suicide Facts at a Glance, Centers for Disease Control and Prevention: http://www.cdc.gov/violenceprevention/pdf/ Suicide_DataSheet-a.pdf.

Chapter 1: Learning Life's Curriculum

1. See Coleman Barks's translations in *Rumi: The Book of Love—Poems of Ecstasy and Longing* (New York: HarperCollins Publishers, 2003).

Chapter 2: Hell No!

1. See Coleman Barks's translations in *Rumi: The Big Red Book— The Great Masterpiece Celebrating Mystical Love and Friendship* (New York: HarperOne, 2010).

Chapter 3: Hell Yes!

1. See Coleman Barks's translations with John Moyne's translations, in *The Essential Rumi,* new expanded edition (New York: HarperCollins, 2004).

Chapter 4: The See Feel Hear Challenge

1. See Coleman Barks's translations in *Rumi: The Big Red Book—
    The Great Masterpiece Celebrating Mystical Love and Friendship*
    (New York: HarperOne, 2010).

Chapter 5: The Power of the Heart

1. See Coleman Barks's translations in *Rumi: The Big Red Book—
    The Great Masterpiece Celebrating Mystical Love and Friendship*
    (New York: HarperOne, 2010).

2. World Health Organization, Preamble to the Constitution
    of the World Health Organization as adopted by the
    International Health Conference, New York, June 19–22,
    1946; signed on July 22, 1946, by the representatives of 61
    States (Official Records of the World Health Organization,
    no. 2, p. 100) and entered into force on April 7, 1948.

3. See Rollin McCraty's book *The Energetic Heart:
    Bioelectromagnetic Interactions Within and Between People*
    (2003). McCraty is director of research at Institute
    of HeartMath, and the booklet is available at
    www.heartmath.org.

4. See Rollin McCraty, Mike Atkinson, Dana Tomasino, and
    William A. Tiller's paper "The Electricity of Touch: Detection
    and Measurement of Cardiac Energy Exchange Between
    People" in *Brain and Values: Is a Biological Science of Values
    Possible?*, edited by Karl H. Pribram, pp. 359–79 (Mahwah,
    NJ: Lawrence Erlbaum Associates, 1998). Available at www
    .hearthmath.org.

5. See David Hawkins's book *Power vs. Force: The Hidden
    Determinants of Human Behavior* (Carlsbad, CA: Hay House,
    2002).

6. See Norman MacLean and Brian Keith Hall's book *Cell Commitment and Differentiation* (New York: Cambridge University Press, 1987).

Chapter 6: The Mind as a Tool for Change

1. See Coleman Barks's translations in *The Soul of Rumi: A New Collection of Ecstatic Poems* (New York: HarperOne, 2001).

2. Penrose, Sir Roger. *Shadows of the Mind: A Search for the Missing Science of Consciousness* (Oxford, UK: Oxford University Press, 1994).

Chapter 7: What's Wrong with Now?

1. See Coleman Barks's translations in *Rumi: The Big Red Book— The Great Masterpiece Celebrating Mystical Love and Friendship* (New York: HarperOne, 2010).

2. See Eckhart Tolle's book *The Power of Now: A Guide to Spiritual Enlightenment* (Novato, CA: New World Library, 1999).

3. See Vinoth K. Ranganathan, Vlodek Siemionow, Jing Z. Liu, Vinod Sahgal, and Guang H. Yue's paper "From Mental Power to Muscle Power—Gaining Strength by Using the Mind," in *Neuropsychologia*, vol. 42 (7): pp. 944–956 (2004).

4. See Candace Pert's book *Molecules of Emotion: Why You Feel the Way You Feel* (New York: Scribner, 1997).

Chapter 8: The Mind as a Tormentor

1. Coleman Barks, translator, with John Moyne, A. A. Arberry, and Reynold Nicholson, *The Essential Rumi* (San Francisco, CA: Harper, 1995).

2.   See Candace Pert's book *Molecules of Emotion: Why You Feel the Way You Feel* (New York: Scribner, 1997).

Chapter 9: Responsibility and the Freedom to Choose

1.   Coleman Barks, translator, with John Moyne, A. A. Arberry, and Reynold Nicholson, *The Essential Rumi* (San Francisco, CA: Harper, 1995).

Chapter 10: Social Conditioning

1.   See Coleman Barks's translations in *Rumi: The Big Red Book— The Great Masterpiece Celebrating Mystical Love and Friendship* (New York: HarperOne, 2010).

2.   See The Gallup Youth Survey, Knowledge Networks; The Pew Forum on Religion and Public Life, Religious Landscape Survey (2004).

3.   See "Kantar Media Reports U.S. Advertising Expenditures Increased 3 Percent In 2012": http://kantarmediana.com/ intelligence/press/us-advertising-expenditures-increased-3-percent-2012.

4.   See OECD Obesity Update 2012. Organization for Economic Co-operation and Development (OECD): http://www.oecd .org/health/49716427.pdf.

5.   See "The World's Healthiest Countries Bloomberg Rankings": images.businessweek.com/bloomberg/pdfs/WORLDS_ HEALTHIEST_COUNTRIES.pdf.

6.   See Jason Lazarou, Bruce H. Pomeranz, and Paul N. Corey's paper "Incidence of Adverse Drug Reactions in Hospitalized Patients: A

Meta-analysis of Prospective Studies," in Journal of the American Medical Association 279 (15): pp. 1200–1205 (1998).

Chapter 11: Dialoguing with Addiction

1. Coleman Barks, translator, with John Moyne, A. A. Arberry, and Reynold Nicholson, *The Essential Rumi* (San Francisco, CA: Harper, 1995).

2. See the American Society of Addiction Medicine, "Public Policy Statement: Definition of Addiction," p. 1 (2011).

3. See U.S. Department of Health and Human Resources, Substance Abuse and Mental Health Services Administration, "Results from the 2010 National Survey on Drug Use and Health: Summary of National Findings" (2011).

4. See Joshua Freeman's interview of Candace Pert in "The Physics of Emotion: Candace Pert on Feeling Go(o)d," Six Seconds EQ Network (2007), http://www.6seconds.org.

5. See Candace Pert's paper "Neuropeptides: The Emotions and Bodymind," from the Symposium on Consciousness and Survival (Institute of Noetic Sciences, 1985).

6. See note 4 above.

7. See "Treatment of Drug Abuse and Addiction: Part III," *Harvard Mental Health Letter,* vol. 12 (4), October 1995.

8. See Dr. David R. Hawkins's book *Power vs. Force: The Hidden Determinants of Human Behavior* (Carlsbad, CA: Hay House, 2002).

9. See "Obscenity and the First Amendment," Statement of Janet M. Larue, Chief Counsel, Concerned Women for America, Summit on Pornography, Washington, DC (May 19, 2005).

10. See "Pornography: Quick Facts: Reliable and Informative Snapshots of the Focus Issue," The Ethics & Religious Liberty Commission: http://erlc.com/issues/quick-facts/por/.

11. See Pornography Statistics, Enough Is Enough (EIE): http://www.internetsafety101.org/Pornographystatistics.htm.

Chapter 12: Getting from Here to There

1. Coleman Barks, translator, with John Moyne, A. A. Arberry, and Reynold Nicholson, *The Essential Rumi* (San Francisco, CA: Harper, 1995).

Chapter 13: Questions About the See Feel Hear Challenge

1. Coleman Barks, translator, with John Moyne, A. A. Arberry, and Reynold Nicholson, *The Essential Rumi* (San Francisco, CA: Harper, 1995).

Chapter 14: Questions about the See Feel Hear Challenge and the Mind and Body

1. Coleman Barks, translator, with John Moyne, A. A. Arberry, and Reynold Nicholson, *The Essential Rumi* (San Francisco, CA: Harper, 1995).

2. The National Cancer Institute, SEER Stat Fact Sheet from the The Surveillance, Epidemiology, and End Results (SEER) Program.

3. See the World Research Foundation, "The Power of Mind and the Promise of Placebo," www.wrf.org.

Chapter 15: The Heart's Unprocessed Beliefs— The HUB for Discovering Gifts in Strange Wrapping Paper

1. Coleman Barks, translator, with John Moyne, A. A. Arberry, and Reynold Nicholson, *The Essential Rumi* (San Francisco, CA: Harper, 1995).

ACKNOWLEDGMENTS

There are way too many people to list who deserve thanks for the creation of *The Heart of the Matter,* but we'll give it our best shot. First off, thanks to the serendipitous Universe for bringing us together to write this book. It's been a blast!

Thanks to the friends, family members, and thousands of people who have trusted Darren along their journey of conscious awakening. Darren says, "I'm forever blessed for having the pleasure and honor of being a part of your healing path. Infinite Love & Gratitude to all of you!"

Both of us want to thank the amazing editorial team at Hay House, Alex Freemon and Patrick Gabrysiak; creative director Christy Salinas; and the other wonderful family members at Hay House. Thank you for helping us to craft this beautiful book. You are all such a pleasure to work with.

Infinite Love & Gratitude to Dr. Bruce Lipton for honoring us by writing the Foreword. Your presence in the world has enlightened and awakened humanity to what's possible when we choose it.

A big thank you to Coleman Barks who gave us permission to include his wonderful Rumi translations at the beginning of each chapter. They add so much! Thank you to Shelley Lucas, who made our graphics come alive, and to photographer Barbra Kates, who played the Photoshop game with us!

On a more personal note from Darren: "Thank you to my mom and dad for being you. I love you both so very much. To Sarit, Joya, Rumi, and Liam Weissman, I am forever blessed to share every day with you in *The Heart of the Matter*. You are gifts in beautiful wrapping paper. Your love and support fuel my passion to shine even brighter! Infinite Love & Gratitude."

❧

ABOUT THE AUTHORS

Dr. Darren R. Weissman is the developer of The LifeLine Technique, a practical, everyday, leading-edge system of holistic healing that aligns the conscious and subconscious minds to enable you to live in the present moment. One of the primary philosophies of The LifeLine Technique is that pain, fear, and stress are emotional signals stemming from the subconscious mind—a secret code that empowers you to awaken your fullest potential for healing and your best self for embracing life's stressors. Darren received his undergraduate degree at Kansas University, and went on to receive his BS in human biology and doctorate of chiropractic from the National College of Chiropractic. He received additional intensive training in acupuncture, homeopathy, and other forms of energy-based medicine at the Kalubowila Teaching Hospital in Colombo, Sri Lanka.

Darren's other postgraduate studies have included applied kinesiology (AK), Total Body Modification (TBM), Neuro Emotional Technique (NET), neuro-linguistic programming (NLP), NeuroModulation Technique (NMT), Chinese energetic medicine, natural healing, and many others that finally led to his developing a complete system of mind-body-spirit healing called The LifeLine Technique. In addition to serving as director for his private practice, The Infinite Love & Gratitude Wellness Center in Northbrook, Illinois, Darren also continues to instruct and certify people from all over the world as Certified LifeLine Practitioners (CLPs). There are CLPs in over 14 countries around the world and growing strong.

❦

Cate Montana is the author of *Unearthing Venus: My Search for the Woman Within* (September 2013) and a co-author of *GhettoPhysics: Redefining the Game* with *What the Bleep Do We Know!?* creator Will Arntz. Cate's work focuses on self-realization, the physics of consciousness, and implementing feminine life values and sustainable lifestyles.

Former publisher of the online magazines *The Global Intelligencer* and the wildly popular *Bleeping Herald* for the international hit film *What the Bleep Do We Know!?*, Cate has published hundreds of articles in the mainstream media, including the *Seattle Post-Intelligencer* and *Seattle Magazine*. She also worked as Northwest bureau chief for the national Native American newspaper *Indian Country Today.* Prior to her writing and publishing career, Ms. Montana freelanced as a videotape editor for U.S., European, and Canadian television networks.

Co-author of the screenplay *Zentropy,* which is currently in preproduction with Hollywood filmmaker Betsy Chasse, Cate is also the author of the screenplay *The Return,* a spiritual thriller, and the film adaptation of *A Gathering of Selves,* the spiritual adventures of Alvin Schwartz, real-life creator of Superman and Batman for Detective Comics. Currently, Cate is writing a book called *A Love Beyond the Pale* and developing seminars about feminine empowerment. She lives in the Pacific Northwest.

❦

NOTES

NOTES

NOTES

NOTES

NOTES

Hay House Titles of Related Interest

All of the above are available at your local bookstore,
or may be ordered by contacting Hay House (see next page).

❧

We hope you enjoyed this Hay House book. If you'd like to receive our online catalog featuring additional information on Hay House books and products, or if you'd like to find out more about the Hay Foundation, please contact:

Hay House, Inc., P.O. Box 5100, Carlsbad, CA 92018-5100
(760) 431-7695 or (800) 654-5126
(760) 431-6948 (fax) or (800) 650-5115 (fax)
www.hayhouse.com® • **www.hayfoundation.org**

Published and distributed in Australia by: Hay House Australia Pty. Ltd., 18/36 Ralph St., Alexandria NSW 2015 • *Phone:* 612-9669-4299 *Fax:* 612-9669-4144 • www.hayhouse.com.au

Published and distributed in the United Kingdom by: Hay House UK, Ltd., Astley House, 33 Notting Hill Gate, London W11 3JQ • *Phone:* 44-20-3675-2450 • *Fax:* 44-20-3675-2451 • www.hayhouse.co.uk

Published and distributed in the Republic of South Africa by: Hay House SA (Pty), Ltd., P.O. Box 990, Witkoppen 2068 • *Phone/Fax:* 27-11-467-8904 • www.hayhouse.co.za

Published in India by: Hay House Publishers India, Muskaan Complex, Plot No. 3, B-2, Vasant Kunj, New Delhi 110 070 • *Phone:* 91-11-4176-1620 • *Fax:* 91-11-4176-1630 • www.hayhouse.co.in

Distributed in Canada by: Raincoast, 9050 Shaughnessy St., Vancouver, B.C. V6P 6E5 • *Phone:* (604) 323-7100 *Fax:* (604) 323-2600 • www.raincoast.com

Take Your Soul on a Vacation

Visit **www.HealYourLife.com®** to regroup, recharge, and reconnect with your own magnificence.
Featuring blogs, mind-body-spirit news, and life-changing wisdom from Louise Hay and friends.

Visit **www.HealYourLife.com** today!

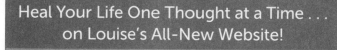
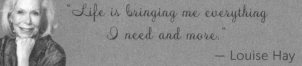